The Opulent Era

FASHIONS OF WORTH, DOUCET AND PINGAT

The Opulent Era

FASHIONS OF WORTH, DOUCET AND PINGAT

Elizabeth Ann Coleman

THAMES AND HUDSON
AND THE BROOKLYN MUSEUM

This book accompanies an exhibition organized by
The Brooklyn Museum.
December 1, 1989–February 26, 1990

First published in hardcover in the United States in
1989 by Thames and Hudson Inc.,
500 Fifth Avenue, New York, New York 10110

Library of Congress Catalog Card Number 89-50545

Printed and bound in Singapore

Contents

FOREWORD

Nearly thirty years ago The Brooklyn Museum presented a ground-breaking exhibition focusing on the House of Worth. Such was the impact of this exhibition and accompanying monograph that to this day the names of Worth and The Brooklyn Museum are still closely associated. In view of the growth of the Museum's impressive collection of historical haute couture attire, advances in scholarship, and the lapse of time, it is appropriate to review the most remarkable garments of an era when Paris was the undisputed capital of fashion—the end of the nineteenth century.

The present undertaking not only focuses on the House of Worth, but also compares and contrasts the couture establishments of two other notable contemporaneous purveyors of *la mode*: Doucet and Pingat. This is the first time attention has been drawn to the works of these houses, and it is hoped that the exposure will encourage additional reviews of the creative vocabulary of late nineteenth- to early twentieth-century attire by master couturiers. As our own century draws to its conclusion, we can see just how much, and how little, sensibilities have changed in a brief one hundred years. Glitter still draws attention, but radical distortion of the female figure and incumbering layers of fabric are outmoded.

I want to extend my appreciation to all who have generously contributed to the endeavor. Lenders to the exhibition have shared extremely fragile garments, including some whose condition will prevent future exposure. This project has been the constant companion for several years of the Museum's Curator of Costumes and Textiles, Elizabeth Ann Coleman, and her staff, particularly Carol Dean Krute. Acknowledgment for the financial support essential to the realization of this project is gratefully extended to the National Endowment for the Arts, and to the William Randolph Hearst Foundation.

Robert T. Buck, Director

INTRODUCTION

It was the internationally held feminine fantasy of the second half of the nineteenth century to be dressed in a Worth creation. Conversely, it was a Worth fashion fantasy to dress the world. While neither achieved its goal, the House of Worth was for two generations viewed as *the* place to acquire luxury garments, especially evening, bridal and court attire. By World War I the house's influence was in sharp decline, having been superseded by a young, talented, and audacious former design assistant, Paul Poiret. He breathed life into garments that the Worth sons—the business and creative heirs of the house's founder, Charles Frederick—could not match. From his own flock of contemporaries the senior Worth's continuing challenge came from one source, a now forgotten man by the name of Emile Pingat. Almost paralleling the careers of the two younger Worths—Gaston and Jean-Philippe—was a third generation Doucet, Jacques, whose family had contributed to wardrobes since about 1816.

All three Parisian couture houses bear certain distinct characteristics, yet in rare instances confusion of attribution may arise. The House of Worth garment designs at the fin de siècle are inseparable from the fabrics they employed. More than either Worth or Doucet the creations of Pingat reflect a flirtation with non-traditional western European patterns, a perfection of construction techniques and mastery of outer garments. Worth excelled at overstatement, sometimes extending ostentation into the realm of vulgarity. The house produced a series of remarkably limited basic design foundations, and fabrics of unsurpassed quality. Its confections display a liking for historical interpretations both in fabrics and fashions. The much quieter Doucet whispers in pastel shades decked with laces, reflecting the family's long established association with the finest linens, laces and embroidery. Jacques Doucet's personal focus on the eighteenth century is translated into numerous garments.

It is the intention of this publication to discuss the creations of the three houses as they relate to everyday attire. Theatrical fashions will be considered only as they reflect ordinary fashions and fancy dress ensembles will not be discussed.

Time and money have been exhausted in preparing this project. However, energy and enthusiasm remain for continuing down all the paths opened by researches. Regretfully not all creations of the Houses of Worth, Pingat and Doucet dating prior to 1905 have been traced or documented. Contents of many major public collections on both sides of the Atlantic have been explored, all yielding great quantities of Worths in proportion to Doucets and Pingats. Some items examined were discarded as not being authentic, usually because the garment did not live up to the total construction vocabulary of the house in question. Other unlabeled fabrications were judged valid because of sufficient house signature elements. An appended house label does not guarantee authenticity: it could have been removed from another garment or was judged a downright forgery (see pp. 84, 85, 88, 89; house labels are arranged chronologically in the text and are augmented with spurious and related examples).

Colleagues have offered support, guidance, and good humor. I trust their faith in the outcome of this project begins to be fulfilled and that all interested in a fascinating aspect of a rich moment in time will find some new nugget revealed. Acknowledging contributions hardly begins to express my sincere gratitude to so many who went out of their way to be of assistance, but the following opened a variety of important doors—to libraries, to storerooms, and in the mind: (Cincinnati Art Museum) Otto Charles Thieme; (Cooper-Hewitt) Gillian Moss; (Fashion Institute of Technology) Laura Sinderbrand; (Fine Arts Museum of San Francisco, M. H. de Young Memorial Museum) Melissa Leventon; (Cora Ginsburg, Inc.) Cora Ginsburg; (Kyoto Costume Institute) Jun Kanai; (Los Angeles County Museum of Art) Dale Gluckman and Sandra Rosenbaum; (The Metropolitan Museum of Art) Jean Druesedow, Kimberly Fink, and Robert Kaufmann, Costume Institute, and Alice Zrebiec, Textile Study Room; (Musée des Arts Décoratifs) Barbara Spadiccini-Day and Nadine Gasc; (Musée de la Mode et du Costume) Guillaume Garnier, Françoise Tetart-Vittu and Fabienne Falleul; (Museum of Costume, Bath) Penelope Byrde; (Museum of Fine Arts, Boston) Jean-Michel Tuchscherer and Deborah Kraak; (Museum of London) Kay Staniland; (Museum of the City of New York) JoAnne Olian and Phyllis Magidson; (Philadelphia Museum of Art) Dilys Blum; (Phoenix Art Museum) Jean Hildreth; (Rhode Island School of Design) Susan Anderson Hay; (Royal Museum of Scotland) Naomi Tarrant; (Smithsonian Institution) Claudia Kidwell; (Union Française des Arts du Costume) Florence Muller; (Victoria and Albert Museum) Madeleine Ginsburg and Avril Hart.

Lynton Gardiner photographically captured many of the figures. Elizabeth Jachimowicz of the Chicago Historical Society, Martin Kamer, and Janet Arnold assisted with much-needed expertise. Late twentieth-century word-processing technology under the tutelage of Richard Nagley was employed and where the machines and I failed, Joanna Ekman was there to edit the manuscript.

Any endeavor is a shared accomplishment. The various departments of the Museum offered their finely honed professional assistance along the way: Robert T. Buck, Director; Barbara McMahon, Development Manager; Robin Rosenbluth, Foundation Development Associate; Linda Ferber, Chief Curator; Kenneth Moser, Chief Conservator; Cathryn Anders, Collections Manager; Barbara LaSalle and Elizabeth Reynolds, Registrars; Jeffrey Strean, Chief Exhibition Designer; Richard Waller, Chief Designer; Elaine Koss, Assistant Director for Publications; Rena Zurofsky, Vice Director for Marketing; Missy Sullivan, Manager, Public Programs; Pat Bazelon and Patty Wallace, Chief Photographer and Photographic Technician. The conservation-related tasks of preparing the garments for exhibition and photography were filled admirably by Debora Jackson and Edle Lieberman while Departmental Assistant Denise Watkins provided secretarial support. Behind all of the above and always there for me was Carol Krute.

Elizabeth Ann Coleman, Curator

1

The House of Worth

❧❧❧❧❧❧❧❧❧

THE HOUSE

During the second half of the nineteenth century, the honor of ultimate fashion arbiter was bestowed upon the English-born dressmaker Charles Frederick Worth (1825–95). The house he coestablished in 1857 at 7 rue de la Paix in Paris was sought out by the rich, the royal, and the raffish as if it possessed the curative powers of some rejuvenating shrine.

Boldness in all approaches to personal packaging seems an appropriate way to sum up the style of Charles Frederick Worth. He fancied himself an artist, dressing accordingly and on occasion going so far as to assume a slight variant of the attire that Rembrandt (fig. 1.1) had chosen for one of his self-portraits.[1] Handicaps like a lack of linguistic facility did not throw Worth off course—indeed, that failing may ultimately have worked to his advantage. Worth's achievement was that he conquered a foreign profession in a foreign land, captivating many English-speaking clients in their common language.

Worth was born on October 13, 1825, in Bourne, Lincolnshire. While he came from a family of solicitors, it is said that his family chose the printing trade for young Charles, who took exception to the plan because he disliked soiling his fingers with printer's ink. As his father was a drinker, the rearing of Charles and his one surviving sibling was left to his mother, who apparently packed the adolescent off to London in the spring of 1838. Just where Worth began his career is unknown, but he has been associated with two well-known dry-goods firms. His apprenticeship may have been served at Swan & Edgar, where "he developed and perfected his appreciation of the productions of the French milliners and dressmakers, superintending the unpacking of every case of pattern garments that arrived."[2] However, Worth's son Jean-Philippe (1856–1926) claimed that his father worked with London's most exclusive silk mercers, Lewis and Allenby, who had recently been styled purveyors to Queen Victoria. Charles Frederick is believed to have left the employ of Lewis and Allenby, for whom he worked for some time in 1845–46,

Stamped gold on white petersham
c. 1863–67

1.1 Charles Frederick Worth, the artistic autocrat of fashion, from an engraving based on a photograph by Felix Nadar of early 1892. Worth is seen assuming the apparel of artists—beret and smock—and striking a Rembrandt-like pose.

to further his career in Paris. Allenby was to maintain contact with Worth, visiting with him on buying trips to Paris, and this personal association may be one reason why, even as late as the mid-1890s, Lewis and Allenby sold Worth garments in connection with their own house label.[3]

Much mythology of struggle and poverty surrounds Worth's first year or so in Paris. Jean-Philippe, in a rare down-to-earth moment in his memoir, *A Century of Fashion*, says his father may have entered trade in Paris as a shop assistant at La Ville de Paris, a dry-goods establishment. It was not long after Worth's arrival in Paris that he was taken on at Gagelin-Opigez et Cie as a selling clerk.[4] We may conjecture how Worth came to work for this firm, since Opigez is credited in the 1847 Didot-Bottin Paris trade directory with having additional establishments in Lyon and London (although there is no entry in *Kelly's Postal Directory* for London). Surely as an aggressive young man,

1.2, 1.3 Dress and fabric of the type associated with Gagelin-Opigez et Cie. Fabric woven *en disposition*, or specifically for making up, as skirt flounces. Lyonnaise appled green patterned silk taffeta dated to c. 1855.: The specifications for such goods. The Brooklyn Museum, Gift of Mrs. H. M. Burrell, 28.71; Private Collection.

Worth would have scouted a Paris-based competitor prior to setting out for France. Or perhaps he was friendly with members of his own generation in the Opigez and Gagelin families.

Gagelin-Opigez was perhaps the most widely diversified clothing establishment in Paris, and although it seems to have specialized in shawls and wraps, other objects of dress and dressmaking supplies were on hand. It advertised that it manufactured and distributed ''hautes nouveautés, broderies de l'Inde, articles de goût,'' and it handled ''soieries et câchemires'' (highest quality fancy goods, Indian embroideries, tasteful articles, silks and shawls). The company's main achievement in the early 1850s was to bring home the only gold medal for dressmaking from the 1851 Crystal Palace exhibition in London (figs. 1.2, 1.3). The entry included ready-made articles for ladies: rich Lyon silk, embroidered fabrics, shawls, and cashmeres. The jury report critiques the fabrics—exceptional embroidered silks—more than the fashions, the dresses of elegant style. Just what, if anything, of his own design Worth contributed to this display is unknown.

At the end of 1851 a political event took place that would eventually have a profound impact on the career of the young Worth. On December 2, 1851, Louis Napoleon Bonaparte (1808–73) succeeded in his third attempted coup d'état. A plebiscite validated his actions, and he proclaimed the French Empire restored in 1852. As Napoleon III, Louis Napoleon took several lessons from his uncle, Napoleon I. Paris should be a city of ceremony and the imperial court one of display. In January 1853 the new emperor was married to Eugénie de Montijo de Guzman (1826–1920), a Spanish countess of mixed Scottish-Spanish descent and with slightly exotic features. It is said that at the time of the imperial marriage Gagelin had supplied some of the fabrics that found their way into Eugénie's trousseau.

During the early 1850s Worth is believed to have begun creating dresses for Gagelin. Under the Second Empire, garments for wear at court again became important, and to acknowledge this renewed aspect of dress at the 1855 Exposition Universelle, Gagelin-Opigez entered a selection of fashionable novelties, court trains, and designs for reproduction.[5] It was one of these court trains that took the first-class medal under class 25—"Confection des articles de vêtement; Fabrication des objets de mode et de fantaisie." Designed by Worth, the train was white watered silk embroidered in gold, and even the worked motif was a Worth creation. At the time of its fabrication, it was so sumptuous that a valuation of $3,000 was not considered unwarranted. New in construction, the train was suspended from the shoulder rather than from the waist, thus providing a greater sweep of fabric on which decorative motifs could be applied.

The Times of London, in Worth's obituary, records that he applied for a share in the Gagelin business soon after the success of the exhibition, but was refused.[6] Other chroniclers maintain that he tried to set up a dressmaking department in the firm, though contemporary evidence indicates that such a department had been long established. Whatever the scenario, Worth must have felt constrained and eager to move ahead.

By this time Worth was married to Marie Augustine Vernet (1825–98), another Gagelin employee, and had a growing family. The designer, together with his wife, decided to look for a suitable business site, and one with living quarters attached for the Worth family. In partnership with another alien, the Swede Otto Gustaf (Gustave) Bobergh (1821–81) (fig. 1.4), he set up business on the first floor, one flight up, at 7 rue de la Paix,[7] and they began trade in the autumn/winter of 1857–58, as "Worth and Bobergh." Estimates of the initial staff range from fewer than twenty, to fifty workers.[8] By 1860 the business was listed in the Paris trade directory as "Worth and Bobergh,

1.4   Otto Gustave Bobergh, partner in Worth and Bobergh from 1857 to 1870.

Maison Spéciale, Robes et Manteaux, Confectionnés, soieries, haute nouveautés, Paix 7," with additional listings under "couturiers" and "nouveautés confectionnées."[9] Soon claims were made that more than a thousand
workers assisted in the fabrications. The scale of operation probably included
several outside workshops, which made up orders on command. In 1869 and
1870 Worth and Bobergh are listed as purveyors to Their Serene Majesties
the Empress of France and the Queen of Sweden and Norway.

The partnership lasted until 1870–71; the circumstances surrounding the
separation are unknown. One client reports that Worth did most of the brain
work and Bobergh was the "sleepy" partner.[10] But unlike Worth, Bobergh
knew how to handle money. The son of a banker, he is thought to have
contributed the majority of the financial backing for the business, while
Worth provided most of the creative skills and showmanship. Otto Bobergh
had much in common with Worth and some unique qualities to offer in their
joint venture. He had received an art education in Stockholm that refined his
talents as a sketch artist. The schooling had focused his eye on the treasures of
picture collections, just as Worth's studies in the great art galleries of the
Louvre in Paris and the National Gallery in London had familiarized him
with fashions from the past. Bobergh, too, had worked in dry-goods
establishments in London before heading for Paris in 1855 for wider
experience. There he received supplementary training in merchandising at
another major dry-goods emporium, Compagnie Lyonnaise, where he, like
Worth, worked his way up to become a *premier commis*, or head salesman.

A third party was anxious for the success of Worth and Bobergh. Marie
Worth, continuing her career from Gagelin days, acted as model and
saleswoman.[11] It was she who, in 1860, made the first, successful incursion
into the court circle. Thereafter, the fledgling house's success was assured.
The door was opened by the order, for a negotiated total of Fr 600, of two
dresses by the newly arrived and very fashionable Pauline, princess von
Metternich. Wife of the Austrian ambassador, she was as noted for her
unfortunate simian looks as for her taste in dress. Selecting styles from a book
of sketches submitted by Mme Worth, the princess settled on a daytime
outfit and a tulle-draped, floral-festooned evening gown. Worn to the
Tuileries, the evening dress caught Empress Eugénie's eye.

The permutations that could be quickly achieved by draping clouds of tulle
over plain-colored silk taffetas were legion, and such a procedure satisfied the
needs of both a blossoming business and the court (fig. 1.5). It is possible that
all the approximately eighteen garments that the pretty young American
Lillie Moulton packed for her courtly sojourns at Compiègne in 1866 and 1868
were created by Worth: "Invitation received 12 days ago . . . this gave me
plenty of time to order all my dresses, wraps and everything else I needed for
this visit of a week to royalty."[12] For the second visit she enumerates an

1.5 Croquis of Worth ball gown trimmed with wheat sprays, c. 1864. Victoria and Albert Museum, E.22394.1957, p. 55.

afternoon gown, "green faille faced with blue[13] and a red Charlotte Corday sash (Worth's last gasp)," and describes among the six evening dresses a white tulle, embroidered with gold wheat ears—a favorite house motif—that could well have been another Worth confection.[14] While Mrs. Moulton does not mention patronizing any other dressmaker, most women favored one but would acquire supplementary outfits from other establishments.

Although Worth was never the Empress's only supplier, he ensnared the majority of orders for *grandes toilettes* (state and evening wear, court dresses, elaborate street clothes, and masquerade costumes). For ordinary clothes Mme Laferrière was looked to, and Felice[15] produced cloaks and mantles while Mmes Virot and Lebel created millinery. The Englishman Henry Creed was called upon for sportswear, including riding habits.

It was no small undertaking to keep the Empress and her court in clothes. In 1856 *Punch* noted, "The guests are all expected to change their costume twice a day; and no lady is allowed to appear at the Château [Compiègne] twice in the same dress; the Empress setting the example by giving every robe once worn to her attendants. As these are of course sold again, all Paris overflows with the Imperial défroque."[16] In 1863 Mrs. Moulton estimated the value of just the Worth gowns, among the fewer than four hundred ladies at

14

an imperial fancy-dress party held in the Blue Salon, to be $200,000. The simplest Worth dress in 1868 is thought to have cost about Fr 1,600 (about $64). Yet Lillie Moulton seems to complain about the costliness of Worth garments only when discussing her fancy dresses. Once, in early 1863, when she was pleased with results, she wrote: "Worth said that he had put his whole soul in it. I thought he had put a pretty good round price on his soul." A comment of several months earlier regarding a Spanish dancer's toilette reflects her dissatisfaction: "Worth told me that he had put his whole mind upon it; it did not feel much heavier for that: a banal yellow skirt. . . . Some compliments were paid me, but unfortunately not enough to pay the bill . . ."[17] Some have claimed that there were two sets of prices at many of the primary dressmaking houses in Paris, including Worth's: "one for Americans and one for Christians of every other denomination."[18] Addressing the financial arrangements of the house, Jean-Philippe allowed that the majority of its clients paid in cash, or without question met any invoice presented within a year.[19] Some sense of the scale of expenditures may be gained by comparing the annual purchase grant of Fr 7,000 at the disposal of the director of the Louvre in the 1860s against the monthly allowance of Fr 100,000 at the disposal of the Empress.[20]

If the cost of garments was princely, the furnishings and conduct of business at the House of Worth and Bobergh projected an elite image. In 1868 the house was likened to an embassy, staffed with sophisticated young men dressed in black glossy broadcloth, like attachés, with English accents and pearl tiepins, turquoise rings, and curled hair, and working within a grand apartment, heavy with scent and rich elegance. In the yard-goods salons, activities were directed by a *premier commis* named Isidor Carlsson who, like Bobergh, was a Swede. His activities found approbation with princess von Metternich, who thought he handled his position splendidly.

At mid-century, the number of talented males entering the upper echelons of the clothing business had risen, following a decline over the previous twenty-five years. Beginning business almost simultaneously with Worth were two lifelong competitors, Felix and Pingat. In 1863, Charles Dickens noted the change: "Would you believe that, in the latter half of the nineteenth century, there are bearded milliners—men-milliners, authentic men, like Zouaves—who, with their solid fingers, take the exact measurements of the highest titled women in Paris—robe them, unrobe them, and make them turn backwards and forward before them."[21]

Entering a *maison de couture* was like crossing the threshold of some handsome private residence. It did not beckon to the casual wanderer, but was approached with due formality, with the feeling that credentials or an introduction from a patron was necessary. One observer saw the whole business establishment at Worth, including the family's apartment, as exuding "some atmosphere of degraded aristocracy, some heady fragrance of elegance, wealth and forbidden fruit."[22] Most couture houses were inconspicuously identified with gilt lettering at the door. Within were spacious and beautifully furnished salons, from which one was personally conducted to the display rooms. Word of mouth drew clients; the house did little direct advertising (fig. 1.6). In 1868 Joseph Primoli, a nephew of Princess Mathilde, wrote of a visit to Worth's: "I have been with mother to Worth's. He is the great couturier in fashion. He charges sixteen hundred francs for a simple little costume! Ladies arrange to meet at Worth's and they talk politics as they sip tea. At Worth's, the faubourg Saint Germain sits between two kept women, and the world of officialdom meets the faubourg Saint Germain. Perhaps M. Worth does not even realize what he is doing, but he is reconciling all political parties and mingling all social classes."[23] The House of Worth was such a popular and fashionable spot that the staircase leading to the salons was likened to Jacob's Ladder, with an angel on every step.

In 1867 Bostonians Isabella Stewart Gardner and her husband, Jack, on one of their near-perennial European jaunts, mounted the house's crimson-carpeted stairs, banked on each side with flowers. They first entered a room where nothing was displayed but black and white silks—as if to clear the palate in this palace of temptation. Eyes then focused on the real decor of the room set off by the yards of austere yet startling fabrics. Nestled in were excessively overstuffed chairs and couches, and glass and gold-leaf curio cabinets revealing enchanting bits of Mr. Worth's private collection. Here one could only look at the snuffboxes and antique fans: they were not for sale. Next came the rainbow room, with silks in all colors, almost liquid, from the looms of Lyon, except for some imported Italian brocades that Worth fancied. The third room, like a padded cell, contained the pile fabrics: velvets, plushes, and the like. Then came the austere yet robust woolen goods, many of British finishing. Having undergone the visual and tactile experiences offered by these ante-showrooms, one was now prepared to enter another salon where actual garments were displayed on wooden forms. A mirrored wall surround immediately put the customer in the picture in an obvious attempt to contrast the freshness of the model creations with the reflections of their own fading fashions.[24] Later, a "salon de lumière" was specially outfitted with mirrors and gaslight to simulate an evening ambience, so that clients could see the effect of gowns worn in those hours.[25]

The salons were comfortable yet, like the proprietor, somewhat pretentious. In the late 1870s, when Worth alone masterminded the concern, his twin black spaniels would each occupy a green velvet chair in the reception room.[26] Like any good lair, the salons of Worth in the early 1890s boldly proclaimed their raison d'être; with furnishings set off by carpets in imitation tiger skin of gray and black, bordered with scarlet (all described as restrained

1.6 (*Opposite*) Court toilette advertising Maison Worth's gowns and wraps, c. 1872.

16

by one contemporary), the rooms were a perfect artistic den in which to ensnare the victims of fashion.[27] The ambience of the salons, along with the artistic pose of the maestro, prompted concerns for Mme Worth and provided material for satirizing by no less a figure than Hippolyte Taine, who included the Great Worth in his 1867 skit on Parisian life, *Vie et opinions de M. Fréderic-Thomas Graindorge*. Taine's thinly veiled Worth "receives in a velvet jacket, lounging on a divan, cigar in mouth. A society lady comes to him to order a dress. 'Madame,' he asks; 'who has recommended me to you? In order to be dressed by me you have to be introduced. I am an artist with the lone scale of a Delacroix. I compose, and a toilette is just as good as a picture.'" To another client he commands, "Move about, turn around . . . come back in eight days. By that time I will have composed a dress suitable for you."[28] In a similar vein, Felix Whitehurst noted, in 1873: "When this truly great man is composing he reclines on a sofa, and one of the young ladies of the establishment plays Verdi to him. He composes chiefly in the evenings, and says that the rays of the setting sun gild his conceptions."[29] Worth, in an August 1871 interview with F. Adolphus, summed up his autocratic approach: "the women who come to me want to ask for my ideas, not to follow their own. . . . If I tell them they are suited, they need no further evidence. My signature to their gown suffices!"[30] For all his highhandedness, it is said that Charles Frederick Worth took delight not only in superintending all the mechanical and technical aspects of creating the clothing but also in personally supervising the delicate finishing details of a toilette, such as the shaping and trimming of a corsage, the tying of scarves or ribbons, and the placing of artifical flowers on the skirt (fig. 1.7). In floral finishes he must truly have been a magician of *la mode*.

The political events of the early 1870s directly affected operations at Worth. The winter War of 1870 necessitated converting workrooms into emergency wards to receive the overflow from hospitals. For a brief while during the Siege of Paris the house was closed, causing one longstanding client, Marquise de Manzanedo, to wear muslin summer dresses out of season. Even though shipment was difficult during the Commune, the continuing demand of American and British clients encouraged a return to normal activity. Following the fall of the Second Empire and the Franco-Prussian war in 1870–71, there was perhaps more concern and confusion among fashion journalists than fashion designers as to the future of Paris as the epicenter of the trades surrounding haute couture. One author expressed hesitation as to who led the way in fashion, but also wrote: "The vitality of Paris—has already recovered her usual life and animation. Her own 'beau-monde' is absent still, but there is a great affluence of foreigners. Orders pour in from the provinces, and more still from abroad. The recognized arbiters of fashion are constantly written to for information concerning new toilettes,

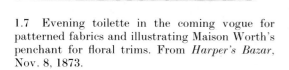

1.7 Evening toilette in the coming vogue for patterned fabrics and illustrating Maison Worth's penchant for floral trims. From *Harper's Bazar*, Nov. 8, 1873.

and 'élégantes' throughout the world come to Paris, hungering, so to speak, after those fashions of which they have been deprived so long."[31] French ladies had "constantly followed in their style of dress the inspiration of True Parisian taste. They have ever openly disapproved the eccentric, theatrical fashions which some ladies from foreign countries, or of the 'demi-monde,' had unhappily brought into great vogue under the influence of certain 'couturiers' of the worst description."[32]

During this time of uncertainty one author, who could envision Worth being driven into exile from the banks of the Seine to those of the Danube in Vienna, observed: "The very doll-shops are devoid of new fashions, and the imagination of milliners must have 'withering fled.' All this, however, is very serious. No doubt extravagance is a vice, luxury a crime, and dress a device unfit for a 'moral republic,' such as that which we now enjoy(?) but I fear I must point out that trade suffers a good deal by our puritanical simplicity.... If Worth sent in, after much and long suffering, big bills, he employed hundreds and expended thousands."[33] The same month this was published, August 1871, F. Adolphus went to interview Worth on this very subject. Business was brisk: there were seventeen persons awaiting the master in nine rooms. According to Jean-Philippe, Charles Frederick Worth had, by helping to revitalize the silk-weaving industry, unwittingly prepared for an easy transition from the days of the Empire to those of the Republic. The Empress had assisted him when she wore a gown of patterned silk fabric woven in Lyon, after a Chinese shawl. This fabric reminded Her Majesty of window-dressing material more than dress cloth, but by publicly promenading in the goods, she sent thousands back to work at the looms of Lyon. An 1872 report projected that there had been a more than doubling of the number of Lyonnaise looms in operation—from 53,500 to 120,000.

Worth apparently did not fare as well during the financial upheavals of the 1880s, although there are conflicting accounts (fig. 1.8). In 1881 political and economic forces conspired against consumption, and entertainments were canceled during the height of the 1881–82 season. Worth, like all other leading dressmakers, made very few ball dresses—simply because demand was gone. Early in 1885, however, it was reported that "the dresses Worth and Felix have turned out lately do not testify to the bad times about which we hear so much when trade is the topic of conversation."[34] Then in 1886, an author wrote that business at Worth had fallen off noticeably, with only a tenth as many workers being employed as before.[35]

In the early 1890s, Nellie Melba relates, the elder Worth had more or less retired and was only to be seen wandering about the great salons, wearing a black skullcap and making occasional suggestions to Jean-Philippe. The second generation (fig. 1.9) of Worths had already begun to assume responsibilities within the house by the middle years of the 1870s. Never

Stamped gold on white petersham. Gothic ampersand, bottom line extends beyond top
c. 1867–70

1.8 The exuberant extravagance of a Worth ball gown, which seems to cascade from the shoulders of its wearer in a manner not unlike money slipping through the fingers. Published in *L'Art et la mode*, 1883.

1.9 The late Charles F. Worth and sons Gaston and Jean-Philippe, headlined among "The Great Dressmakers of Paris." Engraved for the *New York Herald*, April 5, 1896.

Stamped gold on white and black and woven gold on white petersham. Center design smaller on earlier examples
c. 1870–85

questioning career direction as outlined by the paternal "decided despot," the talented Jean-Philippe was nineteen when taken on by his father as a full-fledged employee, the day after receiving his baccalaureate in 1875. His studies had been delayed by the War of 1870, the Commune, and a subsequent lingering illness. Jean-Philippe was to assist his father in aesthetic decisions; his first garments were thirty costumes for the tragedienne Genevieve Ward. The neophyte Jean-Philippe was applauded by his harshest master: "I had fashioned entirely according to my own ideas. I showed them to my father and had the satisfaction of having him declare them perfect—and my father was not given to flattery. Quite the contrary."[36] His brother Gaston-Lucien (1853–1924) was to secure a safer financial future for the company as business manager. Joining the firm about a year earlier Gaston replaced a retiring employee who had been with the company since 1857/58. Gaston was to retain his position as manager and chief cashier until the firm was reorganized after his father's death in 1895, when he assumed additional responsibilities. Of practical temperament and aptitude, he managed to put the spending reins on his father so that investments could be made and capital built up. The business had, from its inception, been operating on a basis of "have it, spend it, hide it under the mattress." Though described in youth as good-looking and charmingly well-mannered, the Worth sons never had the measure of personal flair of their father, and after his unexpected death on March 10, 1895, they were too entrenched in the ways of the past and, perhaps, too aged to revamp the house to keep up with the changing spirit culminating with World War I.

The best years for the house, in financial terms, aside from the initial ones, must have fallen in the decades flanking 1900 (pls. 22, 24). Monied maidens and matrons coveted a Worth confection, whether it was "en gros ou en détail"—ready- or custom-made. Over a brief span in 1895, more than twenty telegrams were received from Madrid, all ordering ball dresses. The house would "make them up as we think fit" and if the clients were long-term, the fittings might well take place on personalized dressmaking figures. Jean-Philippe is quoted in the *Lady's Realm* in 1896: "Of late years the lay [dressmaking] figure has been brought to an extraordinary state of perfection, and, in many cases we have 'mannequins' exactly reproducing our foreign customers' peculiarities of form, etc. Indeed, this system of fitting has many advantages, especially when as not infrequently happens, a client requires twenty to thirty dresses to be made for her at one time. The most successful and newest lay figure is made on the same principle as an India-rubber cushion, and with the help of a pattern bodice, or even the measurements, can be made to express exactly the size and shape required."[37]

By 1897 clients could telephone in an order, send for a mail-order garment, or visit one of the branches in London, Dinard, or Biarritz (a branch was established later in Cannes). It was Gaston's initial idea to have an office, of sorts, in London, where British clientele might come and order gowns to be made in Paris. But London customers wanted more than just a viewing of model gowns, so the office developed to include not only salons where models were shown, but also elaborate workrooms where actual dressmaking took place. The first London establishment opened in 1902–3 at 4 New Burlington Street, but by the 1920s the couture operations were located at 3 Hanover Square,[38] while accessories and the newly introduced house-brand perfumes were offered at 221 Regent Street. Prices were five to ten percent lower because general expenses were down, materials were cheaper, and only a limited number of models had to be displayed. The salons at fashionable resorts were to satisfy customers who might buy accessories as well as gowns, négligés, and even some ready-to-wear apparel. In 1900 the House of Worth, like that of Doucet, is believed to have had a yearly turnover of more than Fr 5 million, and a work force of more than five hundred.

Maison Worth's participation in the 1900 Exposition Universelle in Paris was expected but not guaranteed (figs. 1.10, 1.11), as it was probably the first time Worth-created garments were displayed in such a setting in almost fifty years. Gaston, and more particularly Jean-Philippe, felt the occasion called for an extraordinary arrangement—wax figures in settings. The idea was rejected by fellow couture houses such as Doucet, Paquin, Callot Soeurs, Redfern, Rouff, and Felix, but with persistence, Jean-Philippe transformed a corner of the pavilion into a Louis-XVI-style salon peopled with various Worth fashions, from a maid's outfit to a court-presentation ensemble. The "incidents from English life," as they were called, allowed use of all materials from woolen cloth to brocaded silks, and all styles, from the most elaborate to the uniform of a maid. During World War I the house would be called upon to

1.10   An exhibition confection, with court train. Gown in "Louis XVI sky blue" with fabric woven *en forme*; studded with beads and brilliants, frilled with lace, and layered with flowers. Pictured in *Les Toilettes de la collectivité de la couture* (Paris, 1900).

21

1.11 "Going to the Drawing Room," the Worth display at the 1900 Exposition Universelle.

tailor civilian uniforms—the YWCA overseas ensemble worn by Margaret Merle-Smith, for example, in the collections of the Museum of the City of New York (80.117).

In recognition of various contributions to the French luxury trades, a Légion d'honneur was bestowed in 1901 on Gaston and the house was simultaneously recognized as a NC^t (Ancien Notable Commerçant). The precipitating event had been the grand success of the 1900 Exposition, for which Gaston had been appointed President de Classe, an automatic stepping-stone for the recognition. After the War Jean-Philippe would also be considered for the honor, but he maintained he rejected the award because his father should have received any such honor for the House of Worth and because he felt he could not wear the same award as combatants.

In 1900, not long before the Exposition, a bright young designer previously associated with Doucet was engaged. It is said that Poiret was hired by Gaston, with his eye to the balance sheets, to revive the house. To the young and increasingly flamboyant Poiret, Gaston explained, "We are like some great restaurant, which would refuse to serve aught but truffles. It is, therefore, necessary for us to create a department [under Poiret] for fried potatoes."[39] During his brief two-year stint with Worth, Poiret did produce potatoes, but by 1903 he was on his own. Poiret, who would electrify the fashion world with his colors and fluid garments, observed that he could not flourish in a house that looked to the past for its designs, even if its dresses were masterpieces of artistic beauty and purity.[40] Indeed, the declining influence of Maison Worth had been discussed in the *American Tailor and Cutter* as early as 1897. The author argued that the time was ripe for an American Worth to materialize, and that there was never anything wanted in the United States that was not forthcoming.[41] It was beginning to seem that it had been the senior Worth's independence, above his taste and ingenuity, that had taken the firm to the top.

In 1903 signs of design rigor mortis were recorded of the house, which was described as having "ancient clients, ancient ideas, everything ancient."[42] The Didot-Bottin Paris trade directory for 1904 shows Worth relinquishing space at 7 rue de la Paix. Further evidence of decline is found in the house model photograph albums, now distributed between the Victoria and Albert Museum and the Museum of Costume, Bath. Both groups show that immediately following the turn of the century there was little design direction and much repetition of creations from up to a decade earlier. Full-capped and leg-of-mutton sleeves in sculptural satins and velvets vie with slimmer silhouette sheaths in mousseline de soie and daintily printed taffetas.

By 1914 the house was dressing more dowagers than debutantes, and many of its most notable clients had died. The House of Worth was no longer setting styles, but merely rubber-stamping others' ideas. In many ways it was a casualty of the War. Gaston, moreover, was broken physically and emotionally by his traumatic wartime experiences. Shattered, he retired from the firm two years after the War ended.

As the first decade of the twentieth century closed, Jean-Philippe had passed on his mantle of chief house designer to his nephew Jean-Charles. Gaston's other son, Jacques, was to follow in the managerial and financial footsteps of his father, serving as another President of the Chambre Syndicale de la Haute Couture Française. It was he who in 1923 began giving paid holidays to couture industry workers and oversaw the foundation of a trade school, Ecole Supérieur de la Couture, in 1930 (figs. 1.12, 1.13).

In about 1935 the London branch, located now at 50 Grosvenor Street, was made into a separate business with Elspeth Champcommunal as its designer. This branch was to continue as a privileged customer of the Paris house. Across the Channel, in Paris, Jean-Charles retired as designer, passing on this responsibility to a member of the fourth generation, his nephew Roger, Jacques's eldest son. Roger's brother Maurice followed in paternal footsteps and worked under Jacques in administration of the house, which in 1937 moved to 120 Faubourg St. Honoré. In 1941, upon the death of Jacques Worth, Roger became head of the firm, and after a brief military stint during World War II, Maurice returned as Secretary-General.

1.12   Jean-Charles Worth, son of Gaston and successor to his uncle Jean-Philippe Worth as house designer. Jean-Charles was business partner with his brother Jacques.

1.13   Jacques Worth, son of Gaston and successor to his father as house business manager. Jacques was business partner with his brother Jean-Charles and father of the two sons who closed out the dressmaking business—designer Roger and administrator Maurice.

Beginning in 1952, a series of events signaled the end of the venerable House of Worth. First, Roger retired and was succeeded by Maurice. Then, in 1954, the competing design house of Paquin (founded 1891) bought out Worth in an attempt to reestablish it in the fashion scene, only to close the House of Worth's doors finally two years later. Today the name of Worth lives on through the scents of Parfum Worth.

❧◦❧◦❧◦❧◦❧◦❧

THE WORTH MEN

Like the irregularities of form concealed by the clothes he made, the personality of Charles Frederick Worth is hidden behind his self-serving posturing. To his sons, either intentionally or otherwise, he was an all-commanding figure, both revered and feared for his achievements. To his clients, he was an artist confecting fantasies of fashion with fabrics, furs, feathers, flowers, and fringes. He quite probably saw himself as the actor-artiste who had mastered all aspects of his part. The contemporary world of fashion could not ignore his performance, frequently bestowing rave reviews. From beginning to end, Charles Frederick Worth was a salesman, selling mechanically assembled garments trumped up in the most luxurious materials and trims. Contemporaries have sometimes described him as recessive in nature—but such impressions were probably based on rare and uncharacteristic behavior—and sometimes as volatile and self-centered, qualities far more in keeping with his artistic posturing (figs. 1.14, 1.15).

Although Charles Frederick Worth has been designated the first French couturier,[1] he was born in the English countryside, of strong English stock. He seems never to have relinquished his British citizenship, a privilege he enjoyed through the most golden years of Queen Victoria's reign. It is interesting to speculate on whether he would have changed national allegiances if the Second Empire of France had not ceased. While not overtly promoting the skills and products of England, he is known to have returned to his motherland for holidays and business-associated sojourns.

To one observer, Worth had a "peculiarly low-toned voice with a broad north country accent and very quiet manners."[2] He enjoyed gossipy tales and relished recounting, in vivid detail, anecdotes from his great stock of personal stories of clients, named or unnamed. It was said that he had never been known to lose his patience with even the most exacting and unreasonable of customers but, if pressed too hard by the caprices of any one of them, he would glide quietly away, leaving her to make up her mind before attempting to satisfy. If he did not move away, sometimes his tongue snipped: he is reputed to have advised a very short client who wished to be dressed all in dark green that she would look like an ivy bush.[3]

In 1863, his compatriot Charles Dickens had described Worth as "a perfect gentleman, always fresh shaved, always frizzled, black coat, white cravat and batiste shirt cuffs fastened at the wrists with golden buttons, [who] officiates with all the gravity of a diplomatist."[4] These words were penned before the maestro adopted his own singular style of dressing, which set him apart from the ordinary shopkeeper, including "a cap of black velvet and a cloak or gown of dark material relieved with touches of tulle, and the edges richly trimmed with fur."[5] Dickens saw in the great fashion arbiter a "man-milliner [who] professes to know no distinction nor degree. He is open to all, like the law." Midway in Worth's career, in 1878–79, George Augustus Sala described him as "a man who combines the suavity of a Grandville, the diplomatic address of a Metternich, the firmness of a Wellington and the prompt 'coup d'oeil' of a Napoleon."[6] An unheralded matron could partake of the rejuvenating effects of Worth as readily as any princess. Even through the eyes of some of these matrons, Worth evokes varying reviews. Mrs. Henry Adams (née Marion "Clover" Hooper), in the late 1870s, found "Mr. Worth respectful and sympathetic." She continued, "Alice Mason declared that he is habitually drunk, to which one might retort as Lincoln did, and suggest that a little whiskey of his kind to some other dressmakers might not be amiss."[7]

To receive long-standing clients like Isabella Stewart Gardner[8] of Boston, Worth would don a dressing gown—once it was "puce," or flea-colored. This he wore over his work clothes of a smock and baggy trousers—the traditional garb of the artist—complete with a beret or cap to cover his bald spot. Such attire satisfied the illusion of a creative genius at work. So did his behavior: "He was a most pronounced poseur and his affectations were extravagant almost to grotesqueness. At times he was arbitrary, brusque and even brutally rude. [There was] method in this manner, for through it he secured his own way in everything much more easily than he might have done had his ways been those of courtesy."[9] He maintained that few women had a sense of what was fitting and therefore most needed to be bullied into approving what he designed for them. Indeed he often said that half his time was spent in persuading his customers to abandon what their own hearts were set on and to accept what he chose for them instead.

As a family, the Worths would seem to have been mutually supportive and eccentric only within the established confines of their time. Wed on June 21, 1851, to Marie Augustine Vernet, daughter of an impoverished tax collector from Clermont-Ferrand in the Auvergne and a fellow employee at Gagelin-

1.14 Charles Frederick Worth as a young entrepreneur, c. 1860.

1.15 Charles Frederick Worth attired for winter as a successful entrepreneur. Engraved for *Harper's Bazar*, Jan. 23, 1892.

1.16 Mme Charles F. Worth (née Marie Vernet) and her sons, Jean-Philippe and Gaston, c. 1863. She is seen in the new and controversial short skirt—this example drawn up with interior tapes and known as an elevator skirt. Mme Worth first introduced the skirt and the tieless hat she is seen wearing.

Opigez, Charles Frederick could hardly be accused of marrying above his station (fig. 1.16). During the couple's early years together, there is evidence to suggest that Marie Worth worked as concertedly for the development of the business as her husband did, only retiring in ill-health when two nearly full-grown sons made for an easy transition. According to her wish and church prescription, the sons were brought up in the Catholic church, though Jean-Philippe acknowledged following his father's religion, Church of England. Not overtly religious, nor even a Sunday churchgoer, Charles Frederick would, however, casually drop into houses of worship, and would begin each New Year with silent worship in the local church Sainte-Clothilde. Days were begun with a quarter-hour of reading a biblical chapter. The only concession to Catholicism that Charles Frederick would make was to eat lobsters on Friday. In later years, the senior Worths were doting grandparents, lavishing luxuries, including a skating rink at their country home in Suresnes. The best remembered and favorite grandchild is Andrée Caroline (b. 1881). She was the adored daughter of Jean-Philippe, but the identity of her mother seems a mystery, as it appears her father never married.[10] Andrée's youth was well documented by the great French society and fashion photographers, father and son Félix and Paul Nadar, and in annual portraits by Dagnon-Bouveret. Her marriage in 1898 to Louis Cartier, of the renowned family of jewelers, was one of note, although they divorced in 1900 and Andrée subsequently married M. Jomini.

The Worths had acquired their country villa in 1864. They had proceeded, at vast expense, to enlarge and decorate it, in the manner of their time, converting it into a distinctively ornate, red brick château in the Renaissance style. The construction of the buildings alone had consumed an expenditure of Fr 800,000; yet all trace of the house except a gateway was to vanish within a generation.[11] It was situated in the village of Suresnes, fifteen minutes by hard gallop from the heart of Paris and the rue de la Paix. Commuting from Suresnes, the senior Worth aimed to arrive at his workplace at nine o'clock in the morning, remaining there at least until six in the evening and seldom leaving before seven in the height of the season. (In the early 1890s a second Paris apartment, located at the corner of the Champs Elysées and the rue de Berri, was acquired to cut down on travel between town and country.)

Entry to the grounds at Suresnes was made through a stone gateway in rusticated Renaissance-revival style. The capitals of the flanking pilasters incorporated an aurora behind a hand clasping wings above a scroll. The pedimental urn was flanked by a pair of snails slowly climbing upward, and the iron doors were decorated with cornflowers or bluets. The meaning of these motifs for Worth is now lost, but perhaps the snail was chosen because it can retreat from the world into its own shell—as Worth could do within the oasis of his country house. The capital motif might be interpreted as clasping the wings of fame, on which the sun never set: recognition of Worth's universal fame. As for the cornflowers, they mature through a range of blue, periwinkle, and purple—the colors of success—and they were also a house hallmark found on innumerable fabrics. Those who knew the house describe it as an exotic mixture of Gothic, Indian, English Tudor, and Moorish. The equally fanciful interior was furnished and upholstered throughout from Worth's own designs; even the carpets had been especially fabricated. Acting as his own landscape gardener, Worth ornamented his garden with columns and balustrades rescued from the Tuileries. Although he never was received as the social equal of many of his clients, he entertained them at delightful matinees in town and with an oriental lavishness in the country: "The noble faubourg [Saint-Germain in 1868] aspires to the honor of being received there. The villa, it appears, is full of marvels of every kind. People go there in 'series' as they do to Compiègne!"[12] The marvels of the house included a silver bath in a "cabinet de toilette" and a fountain that is said to have flowed continuously with eau de cologne.

This seeming liking for scent in the environment is contradicted by the observations of two contemporaries. Lucy Hooper noted in 1892: "One personal peculiarity of the great dressmaker deserves special mention, and that is his great dislike to perfumes of any kind. None of his female subordinates are permitted to use scent, or even to wear a rose or carnation or any other richly scented flower during working hours. And when laces are brought to him, all odorous from a long sojourn in perfumery sachets, he has them thoroughly aired before he will occupy himself with their proper arrangement on the dress they are intended to adorn."[13] Edmond de Goncourt has recorded that he felt Worth, whose health was never strong and who frequently suffered debilitating migraine headaches, was incapacitated by the scents deported by his clients. These bouts forced frequent flights from the rue de la Paix to Suresnes, where the pain would prevent Worth from taking a meal.[14]

Princess von Metternich recalled how his indispositions would come most inconveniently just when a fancy toilette was being completed. Once when she arrived for a final fitting, she was informed that M. Worth had retired to his apartment. Rapidly realizing that the staff and seamstresses were "blockheads," unable to give information, the princess, with some courage, climbed up to the second floor, where Worth was living. When she entered his bedchamber, she found him lying on a chaise longue with compresses over his head and eyes.[15]

Princess von Metternich recollected Worth's hospitality at Suresnes under more salubrious circumstances. A tasty snack was presented, either in the garden or in the opulent dining room, with the tea service in vermeil china and the servants in knee breeches and silk stockings. Worth did the honors

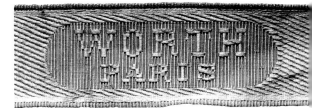

Woven white on white, black on black petersham
c. 1880s–1890s

simply and without affectation; his wife, conversely, put on airs and acted the great lady while their sons stood quietly apart from the group. In 1871, as a dinner guest at Suresnes, F. Adolphus was told, "Of course you won't dress," and remembers his host arriving splattered with mud and foam after horseback riding: "Change of clothes (on the host) brought forth a rusty brown jacket and a battered straw hat without a crown." Mme Worth, however, sat down to dine in "a high but short-sleeved white satin dress, striped with bands of black velvet; a profusion of lace hung over her; long suede gloves reached almost to her shoulders; two or three bracelets were on her arms; a diamond was half hidden here and there in the lace."[16] Even at table, M. Worth kept on the crownless straw hat. The meal was served "in a vast greenhouse which seemed to cover an acre of surface amidst a forest of palm leaves, tree ferns, variegated verdures and fantastic flowers. . . . There was a perplexing mixture of patriarchal simplicity and of the assertiveness of modern money, of thoroughly natural unaffectedness and of showy surroundings, of total carelessness in some things and of infinite white satin in others . . ."[17] Princess Mathilde, a frequent Sunday afternoon teatime guest, saw the house as "ridiculous," preferring a bleached white environment to the excesses of a Worth salon. Nor was princess von Metternich uncritical: "Whilst Worth had taste in everything which concerns the toilette, he lacked it, in my opinion, for everything else, the Villa at Suresnes . . . gave the effect of a confusion of buildings on a site which was much too restricted, all clashing with each other."[18]

As an art collector, Worth was a slavish follower of the collecting and decorating dictates of his time. In marked contrast to Jacques Doucet, he assembled works to impress on scale rather than on refined quality. His collection of ceramics was thought by family members to be one of the largest, if not one of the most valuable, ever established. Edmond de Goncourt, a Sunday teatime guest in 1882, remarked on the collection: "Everywhere on the walls there are plates of every period, and of every country. Mme Worth says there are 25,000 of them, and everywhere, even on the backs of chairs, drops of crystal. It is a delirium of bits of porcelain and carafe stoppers . . . resembling the interior of a kaleidoscope."[19]

Without an understanding of money matters, the senior Worth was headed into a financially insecure future, and family members credit any estate to the prudent judgment of his son Gaston. The spend-all course of the first two decades meant that the wealth the family eventually acquired did not come from the shop, but rather from outside investments, which were made only after Gaston took over management responsibilities beginning in the mid-1870s.

Charles Frederick for years had regarded the tenth of March with foreboding, and the end came on this dreaded date, in 1895. His demise was brought on by a cold, which congested the lungs, and was complicated by a long-term and very serious case of diabetes. Worth probably felt secure that his empire was in the capable, if not as imaginative, hands of his two sons. They, according to Jean-Philippe, had affection enough for their despotic but greatly talented father to take great care not to hurt his feelings by seeming to want to step into his shoes before their time. Walking a delicate line, they were successful in saving his pride. To his dying day he reigned as a great autocrat, living quite removed from the world, except as it sought him out in his salons.

Although the rich and titled intermingled at his funeral, Charles Frederick Worth was buried very simply, in keeping with his beginnings, with Church of England rites held at the Temple de l'Etoile in Paris. He was laid to rest in the family tomb he had planned on his beloved estate at Suresnes, where he would be joined by his wife in three years.

At his death, "le tyran de la mode," as Empress Eugénie had once referred to him, was accorded recognition: "through the length and breadth of the civilized world no contemporary French name is better known than that of Worth; no painter, no sculptor, no poet, no actor, no novelist, of the past three decades has achieved so wide spread a fame as that of this dressmaker."[20] Worth had seized his part and played it unfalteringly: "We live by and for luxury, therefore all questions we ask ourselves are superfluous, we must assume our roles and that is all."[21] Letters of condolence came from the great and the overshadowed. Eugénie wrote of the man, rather than the monarch of fashion: "In my prosperity and in my sorrows he was always my most faithful and devoted friend."[22] Isidor Carlsson, former *premier commis*, sent remembrances from retirement in Sweden, as did two seamstresses, Albertine Debechaux, who had worked with Worth at Gagelin and had followed him to Worth and Bobergh and then to the House of Worth, and an English girl from Godalming who had worked at Maison Worth up to 1879. Official condolences were issued by parties of the textile trade, the Chambre Syndicale des Dentelles et Broderies, and the Chambre de Commerce of Lyon.[23]

Jean-Philippe was a less flamboyant personality but an adept designer. Opera singer Nellie Melba records: "He gave the impression, with his little beard and polished manners, of being a complete Frenchman, and it was difficult to realize his father had been . . . a Manchester boy. . . . I can see him now, placing the tips of his fingers together and half closing his eyes as he examined critically the figure of some woman in need of clothes. He would look at her for some thirty seconds, but he always knew after that brief investigation exactly what dresses she ought to wear." Melba even pronounced: "Jean himself was a greater designer than his father had ever been [fig. 1.17]."[24]

1.17 Jean-Philippe Worth, the artistic director of Maison Worth, c. 1908.

Woven on petersham in various shades of brown on white giving the impression of gold or silver
Various lengths and widths with earliest being longer and wider, later thinner and shorter
Serves Maison Worth under Charles Frederick and Jean-Philippe Worth
Late 1880s on

Ruth Scott Miller, who translated Jean-Philippe's memoir, *A Century of Fashion*, and who had worked on the project during his last months, recalls him as "a man of great dignity, an artist and a connoisseur of rare and beautiful things whose home in the rue Emile Deschanel was filled with collections of furniture, pictures and china of such quality that it elicited a purchase offer from friend, J. Pierpont Morgan." Miller continues that "like many sensitive intuitive souls, it pleased Monsieur Worth to believe that his aspect was intimidating, his features hard, his gaze through his large spectacles frightening and that everyone from the Duchess to the midinette quailed at his approach . . . but he was beloved as one in whom a great deal of the good child has never died."[25]

As a youngster, Jean-Philippe had filled margins of school notebooks with sketches of garments, and his talents were encouraged—even during the Siege of Paris in 1870, when he was permitted to study under the artist Camille Corot, a family friend, on Sundays. These sessions with Corot "were worth at least fifteen years' experience in my own profession and crystallized my flair for drawing into a facility . . . that later was one of my greatest assets."[26] He credited his relationship with Corot with developing his knowledge and love of art, which manifested itself not only in the workplace but also in his private collections at home. Early Corot sketches hung on his walls, but he expressed regret that the senior Worth never was inclined to speculate on the artist's works.

Jean-Philippe was a perfectionist, with an eye for colors more subtle than those his father favored (fig. 1.18). In 1898, one of his evening reception gowns was praised highly: "The picturesque is always in fashion, particularly

for ball gowns—one of Worth's wonderfully combines picturesque and elaborately trimmed . . . [a] gown designed by an artist and [it] is certainly artistic in the best sense of the word."[27] He also received collegial admiration, from no less a figure than Paul Poiret: "But I must say that the dresses which come from the hands of M. Jean were models of art and purity. He worked after the pictures of the old masters, and I have seen him derive magnificent ideas from the canvases of Nattier and Largillière." Poiret went on: "He would make a sleeve out of a long tulle scarf held above the elbow by a row of diamonds and finished by two emerald tassels. (For he could not conceive that a dress could be made without some opulence.) I can understand very well why my little man-in-the-street lucubrations seemed to him wretched and puny."[28]

Jean-Philippe's brother Gaston was born with a great flair for financial affairs and developed a keen interest in the welfare and importance of the dressmaking and couture industries. He was not the public figure both his father and brother had become, but the anchor that kept the firm in business. Unlike Worth senior, who became only one of the vice presidents of the Chambre Syndicale de Nouveautés Confectionnées (1879), Gaston was willing to sit on committees, and served, from 1885 to 1887, as the third president of the Chambre Syndicale de la Couture Parisienne, an organization founded in

1.18 Jean-Philippe Worth, house designer, as characterized for *Femina*, Jan. 1, 1903.

1868 to monitor piracy and act as a self-assistance body for the women's tailoring and ready-to-wear industries. Later Gaston served what seems to be an interrupted term (1894–95, 1897, 1899–1900) as president of La Couturière, a society dedicated to aid workers in the dressmaking trades of Paris (fig. 1.19). In the late 1890s he helped organize—and served as first president of—the Chambre Syndicale de la Haute Couture Française, in an effort to prevent cutthroat rivalry within the profession. Always taking the welfare of workers to heart, he saw to it that those employed by the house were among the first to benefit from insurance and pension schemes. At the request of the "Secretary of Commerce" in the late 1890s he compiled a book of statistics and other data that illuminated the vital commercial significance of the couturier and the importance, if need be, of protecting this seemingly luxury trade. This informative book, *La Couture et la confection des vêtements de femme*, was respected by the entire dressmaking community.

Of the two Worth sons, Gaston was actually more in touch with the trade in which they worked. It was his intense commitment to all things that eventually would spell his early downfall. He was not able to overcome the tragedies of World War I and suffered a severe mental breakdown, wishing to see no one and terrified of noise. Jean-Philippe, who had always lived more in a fantasy world, was the survivor, though by the 1920s he had curtailed his activities in the firm and passed on his duties as head designer to Gaston's son Jean-Charles.

1.19 Gaston Worth, the business manager of Maison Worth, c. 1908.

DISTRIBUTION

The distribution of Worth designs has received almost no attention. Before mapping out some of the channels of circulation yet to be fully explored, we should dispel some commonly held misconceptions. It is, for one thing, a false assumption that all garments with a couture house label were fitted by that house to a specific client. As we shall see, designs were distributed through secondary merchandising sources as well. Nor were garments carrying a label necessarily worn by only one individual. It was the prerogative of many serving-women to royalty and the upper classes to receive cast-off garments. In her recollections, a lady-in-waiting to Eugénie, Mme Carette, wrote: "Twice a year the Empress renewed the greater part of her wardrobe, giving

the discarded ones to her ladies. This was a great source of profit to them because they sold them, generally to people in America and elsewhere, where it is customary to lend toilettes on hire.''[1] Many such garments would end up in the hands of ragpickers—secondhand-clothing vendors—like some Cinderella castoffs (fig. 1.20). Finally, one cannot assume that all garments seemingly identified with a house label are genuine products of that establishment: the label could be spurious or transferred from an authentic article.

With these cautionary words, we may turn to the methods of distribution associated with the House of Worth. Worth had become familiar with distribution techniques while employed at Opegiz-Gagelin. Almost from the outset, he laid the foundation for an enormous export business, in large part generated by American clients who, on returning from their grand tours, inspired envy and desire for emulation among their peers. The essential innovation attributed to Worth does not reside in the cut of his designs; it is, rather, the creative aspect of producing "models," which then could be distributed commercially throughout the world. To this very day it is the presentation of models, many carrying the foreign, exotic names of their creators but first shown under Paris skies, that remains the legacy of Worth, who himself said, "My business is not only to execute but especially to invent. My invention is the secret of my success. I don't want people to invent for themselves; if they did I should lose half my trade."[2] During the 1860s haute couture—the presentation of a collection of models, from which could be

1.20 The ragpickers, or used-clothing dealers, in Paris, as shown in *Le Carreau du Temple*, by Louis Jimenez y Aranda (1845–1904), early 1890s.

33

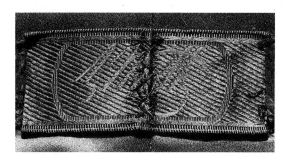

Woven brown on white, gold on black, white
on white, black on black
Generally the cut off middle section of the
previous petersham label
Found on wraps, etc.
Late 1880s on

selected a complete gown or appropriate parts—came to replace *couture à façon*, or dressmaking for the individual. In *couture à façon* the dressmaker had generally been a technician executing an outfit in the fabric and design of the client's preselection. In haute couture, however, the house supplied both the design ideas and the fabric selections, sometimes even having fabrics executed after their own designs. (Maison Worth, unlike nearly all their competitors, specifically and continually advertised that they were silk merchants.)

The leading *modistes*[3] of Europe and America bought garments from Worth to use as models; many of the house's cloaks and gowns were produced with slight modifications many times over. In about 1905, John Wanamaker of Tenth Street, New York City, presented customers with a "Portfolio of Paris Costumes, prepared and published in the interest of our Dressmakers' Supply Department from Exclusive Paris Model Gowns personally selected by our representative in the French Metropolis, and privately exhibited to the Dressmaking Trade." The models, which could be viewed March 7–20, included "Robe Soleil," a costume of pekin gauze ombré stripe in an apricot color, trimmed with steel passementerie and lace. Always missing in the adaptations are house hallmarks, such as fabric; the courage to engage large-scale and bold motifs was a house speciality.

Even within the establishment's own walls, successful models and fabric combinations would be repeated. These might be made up as personalized copies for certain clients, sold directly immediately or at the end of a season, or made up into ready-made costumes. At the end of December 1870 a fashion editor observed, "English ladies are now beginning to find how pleasant and convenient it is, as well as relatively cheap, to buy ready-made costumes, and these are now kept on an extensive scale in all London, as in all Paris, magasins de nouveautés."[4] Costumes based on existing models could be quickly fabricated; in 1895, just before his death, Charles Frederick confided that the house could finish a costume in twenty-four hours, that French ladies had ordered dresses in the morning and danced in them at night, and that on one occasion a gown was finished for Empress Eugénie in three and a half hours. Needless to say, probably none of these gowns involved elaborate decoration or finishing. Another factor behind such rapid production may have been Worth's use of interchangeable parts (see section on Worth's designs).

Export of models may have begun to the United States in the 1860s to establishments such as New York City's then incomparable shopping emporium A. T. Stewart, located on the north east corner of Chambers Street and Broadway. Alexander Turney Stewart (1803–76) made regular transatlantic buying trips for his remarkable department store. In New Orleans an expatriate Frenchwoman, Mme Olympé, began as a milliner in about 1851 and then added a dress department, where she showed both imported creations and those of her own fashioning. She, too, made regular buying trips to Paris and must have been well aware of the House of Worth and its influence, even copying at a very early date its method of labeling garments.

In London in 1873, 97 New Bond Street was tenanted by Princess Bonaparte, wife of Prince Pierre, who had established herself as Mme Pierre Bonaparte, *modiste*, after she and other members of the imperial family were exiled. From her spacious "salons," copies of dresses could be ordered at very moderate prices. A commentator wrote: "I saw some charming confections, models of Worth's designing, lovely lace-trimmed robes, which are pleasant to look upon. . . . The Princess is assisted by an experienced *modiste* long established in Paris, and by a staff of French needlewomen, and merits a success equal to her courage."[5] It is easy to speculate that a sympathetic Worth was behind this establishment and that the princess had been a favored client who had fallen on hard times.

Models by Worth figure in an account by Lady Angela Forbes, daughter of the earl of Roslyn, of her coming out, in about 1893 or 1894, and of the events surrounding it. For a drawing-room reception she had a lovely white dress made by a Mrs. Mason, who imported all her models directly from M. Jean Worth. Lady Forbes was of the opinion that anyone who had any pretensions to dressing well at that time bought copies from Mrs. Mason, although she charged exorbitant prices. (At this time the usual charge for an ordinary silk evening dress from the house in Paris was between fifty and seventy pounds.)

When models for copying and other garments were shipped out by the couturier, the skills of an *emballeur*, or packer, were required (figs. 1.21, 1.22). The practitioner of this Parisian trade could pack "three or four score dresses, each more elaborately trimmed than the other, and of the most fragile materials without crumpling. . . . How lightly he touches the airy fabrics, how daintily he folds them! Large deal boxes are prepared for dresses, which are hung up as in a wardrobe and secured with tape and small tin tacks."[6]

As with bespoken garments there was an afterlife for models acquired for copying. Among the goods sold at reduced prices at the mourning warehouse of Messrs. Jay of Regent Street, London, in 1870, were "French models . . . having been used as designs and not sold by reason of so many ladies requiring varieties in style, quality, or trimming."[7] A year later this London shop was "producing specialities of Parisian costume and chapeaux which are in themselves 'chefs d'oeuvres' of art . . . the exquisite robes and costumes . . . are perhaps not as 'welt famos' as they deserve to be; yet the ateliers of Worth and of Pingat combine in rendering these superb toilettes models of 'haut gout et de distinction'!"[8]

A recently imported model sold in New York during the early 1890s may originally have been brought in for copying, like the models at Messrs. Jay.

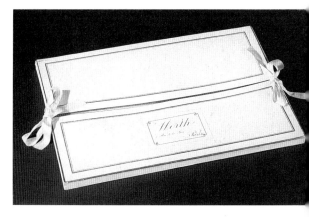

1.21   House of Worth box, c. 1910, The Brooklyn Museum.

IN PARIS.

HE HAS THE OPPORTUNITY OF ENLARGING HIS HORIZON AND OF DEVELOP-
ING AN INTEREST IN THE REAL PURPOSE OF THE TRIP.

1.22 Charles Dana Gibson's *In Paris*, from the series "Mr. Pipps," with dress-packing boxes in the background. As published in *The Gibson Book* (1898), vol. 1.

Because of the rage for picturesque revival gowns at the time, however, it was sold on sight for $300 to an individual.

The first North American citation on the direct copying of a Worth export model seems to belong to New York's Lord & Taylor. In the December 19, 1874, issue of *Harper's Bazar*, their name is attached to an engraving of "a stylish toilette made by the celebrated Paris dressmaker Worth [fig. 1.23]." It is an all-purpose outfit, suitable for wear as an elegant house, dinner, visiting, and evening dress. "The original dress is of black silk, richly trimmed with velvet, silk and fringe." Appealing to spendthrift consumers, the full trained skirt is described as "cut in a new and admirable fashion, which combines gracefulness of effect with great economy of material. It is trimmed with a drapery formed of wings of unequal length, which take the place of an over skirt."

The widely distributed engraving depicts only a high-necked, long-sleeved bodice. Yet with minor variations, plus the addition of a décolleté bodice, this style of garment seems to have been a house workhorse. At least three Worth couture variants survive. The closest to the advertised model is owned by The Metropolitan Museum of Art (fig. 1.24) and has an evening bodice, perhaps the one mentioned but not described or illustrated. Along with it goes a

36

1.23   A stylish, all-purpose Worth outfit imported by Lord & Taylor for the express purpose of copying, as advertised on the cover of *Harper's Bazar*, Dec. 19, 1874.

1.24   Charles F. Worth. *Multifunctional Ensemble*, c. 1874. Peacock blue silk faille; applied border and fringe. Composed of day and evening bodices, skirt and sash. The Metropolitan Museum of Art, Gift of Mrs. Philip Rhinelander, 46.25.1.

streamered belt. The evening bodice for this outfit is an early and almost too perfect example of how the house worked: the lining was ready-made and the outer fabric was quickly draped on for effect; details of fine, or even any, finishing are missing at center-front and center-back waistline, where the evidence of haste would be concealed by the covering layer of the belted sash. To an untrained eye, convinced that perfection in all details is the mark of couture work, this lapse might speak of a butchered attempt at alteration. The less formal basque bodice may have had a fill-in dickey or vestee with a stand collar, which would last as a fashionable feature up until World War I.

It was at the time of this outfit, in the 1870s, that Worth's interest in historical dress extended beyond the limited realm of fancy-dress fantasy to become a pervasive theme in his designs. Skirts, as here, were treated with a tablier, or form-fitting triangular front panel resembling an apron, or the portion of a petticoat that would have been exposed in a seventeenth- or eighteenth-century open-fronted robe. The outfit is densely trimmed, with an elegant banding of deep jewel tones worked in cut pile in a Persian-inspired configuration, set against a white satin ground and bordered with a knotted novelty fringe, which encircles the peacock blue faille of the garment.

1.25 Charles F. Worth. *Reception Dress*, c. 1874. Copper diapered silk twill and pink bengaline, fringe. Worn by Mrs. Manice. Museum of the City of New York, Gift of Mrs. Henry Martyn Alexander, 40.126.1.

1.26 (*Right*) Charles F. Worth. *Reception Dress* with two bodices, c. 1878. Bright blue and pink silk satins and cream-ground pompadour floral stripe; fringe and machine-made lace. Cincinnati Art Museum, Gift of Mrs. Murat Halstead Davidson, 1986.1200.

1.27 Charles F. Worth. *Reception Dress*, c. 1874. Cream ground pompadour floral stripe and green faille; fringe. Worn by Mrs. Stephen de Blois. Wadsworth Atheneum, Hartford, Gift of Mrs. Charles Gregory, Jr., 1969.113.

The House of Worth

A second dress in this manner, in a slightly altered state, is held by the Museum of the City of New York (fig. 1.25). It survives with but one bodice— a sleeved, basque example—and is composed of an unusual twill woven silk faille with a diaper motif in a striking copperish hue, combined with pink *gros de Londrès* ribbed silk. Its skirt may be slightly closer to the Lord & Taylor model, with its sham trim panel, and front tablier with fringed horizontal bands terminating in large rosettes. More distantly related, but still of the genre, is a pompadour striped gown from the collection of the Wadsworth Atheneum (fig. 1.27). The material is a nineteenth-century interpretation of fabric from the previous century. The woven silk floral-sprigged stripes dominate as the asymmetry of dress draping obscures all but a side panel of the banded and fringed tablier.

Local dressmakers not only copied Worth designs, but also made up garments from yard goods handled by the House of Worth—either exclusive designs commissioned by the house, or fabrics also distributed by the textile manufacturers. It is quite probable that several known garments with local dressmaker labels were made up from material that clients had acquired at Worth. The earliest known instance is related to a reception gown of about 1878 in the collection of the Cincinnati Art Museum (fig. 1.26). Belonging

originally to Mrs. Joseph C. Thoms (1847–1936), the outfit has a cuirasse bodice with a modified eighteenth-century center front that incorporates a sham fichu and bastardized stomacher. The cuffed elbow-length sleeves are finished with a flounce of machine bobbin lace, which is repeated around the neckline. Brilliant royal blue silk satin forms the ''robe'' portion of the gown, while the ''stomacher'' and the draped ''petticoat'' are of a delicate 1760s-inspired silk pompadour: pink and green floral sprays scattered between blue stripes on a cream ground. This portion of the outfit carries the Worth house markings. But a matching evening bodice, with short cap sleeves, bears a petersham label from a prominent local dressmaker: ''S. Cadwallader, Cincinnati, Ohio.''

A second probable association is corroborated through rare house documentary photographs of gowns from the late 1880s and early 1890s, among which is found an evening toilette whose silk-ground fabric is embellished with tassel heads. This motif and weaving variants have been found in two collections, but neither has a direct connection with Worth. One example, a skirt panel, of bright gold silk satin sparkled with silver threads, is in the possession of the Museum of the City of New York (see fig. 1.84). The Museum of Fine Arts, Boston, keeps an evening gown constructed from a less flamboyant all-gold corded silk (51.3.21) fashioned in about 1892 by Swann of Newburg.

The house did not achieve the variation in fabrics that it did in garment configuration through its interchangeable pattern parts. In about 1880, at least two prominent Americans were draped in the same fabric, albeit in different colorways. Chicago's Mrs. Cyrus Hall McCormick (née Nancy Maria [Nettie] Fowler) was dressed in a greatly simplified late seventeenth-century-style gown with beige silk faille bodice, hipline band, and train (fig. 1.29). The fabric of the bodice trim and skirt-front panel of cut pile in maroon on a white satin ground reappears, in palest green on a pale aqua ground, on a Boston gown (fig. 1.28). The memorable motif is a tiny leaf chain that undulates between clusters of three plumes caught in a bow.

Despite the range of Worth configurations, it is readily understood why there is also such similarity in Worth garments, let alone fabrics, many of which were unique to the house: for promotional purposes, and no doubt to entice hesitant victims, it was procedure at the house to display models, either on or off live mannequins, and women, along with their prodding spouses or bill-payers, frequently acted like sheep and followed any lead. Several beautiful women paraded before clients arrayed in the latest styles to demonstrate the effect of garments when worn. Marie Worth had been the sole *demoiselle de magasin* (house mannequin) until the mid-1860s, when a bout with bronchitis forced her to retire and other house models were hired to replace her. If a client was expecting a child, there was even, as Edmond de

39

1.28, 1.29   Charles F. Worth. *Reception Dresses*, c. 1880. (*Above*) Pale blue taffeta with white satin patterned with gold-velvet-bowed plume garlands; machine-made lace and fringe; Museum of Fine Arts, Boston, Gift of Mrs. Hugh D. Scott, 50.803. (*Below*) Beige silk faille with white satin patterned with garnet-velvet-bowed plume garlands; machine-made lace. Worn by Mrs. Cyrus McCormick (née Nancy Maria [Nettie] Fowler); Chicago Historical Society, Gift of the McCormick Estates, 1957.1034.

SANDOZ   F. MÉAULLE

Goncourt reported in 1867, "a young lady or rather a woman mannequin, whose specialty is to represent pregnancy in high life. Seated alone at one side, in the half light of a boudoir, she exhibits to the gaze of those visitors in an interesting condition the toilette designed with genius for the ungainly enlargement of being with child."[9] Unfortunately it is not known whether this service inspired Mrs. Stanford White to acquire her brilliant-set black Renaissance velvet ball gown of about 1903 (Museum of the City of New York, 48.306.2).

Except when specially forbidden to do so, it was the practice to place on view wedding dresses created for prominent personages. In the spring of 1880, dresses from the bridal toilette of Collette, daughter of M. and Mme Alexandre Dumas, was already on view in May for a June wedding. The wedding dress was of white Renaissance damask, whose satin ground was covered with large bouquets of roses. Figure-fitting with back lacing, the dress had for its sole trimming a *fraise* (ruff) of white tulle around the throat. For the marriage ceremony to Maurice Lippmann, the bride wore a tulle veil draped with a large bouquet of roses, and a cordon of orange blossoms was fastened at the side.[10]

More private as a bride-elect was a Mlle Blanc who, at the last moment before becoming Princess Roland Bonaparte, informed M. Worth that her trousseau was not to be shown and no exception was to be made to that instruction. According to an apparently unauthorized account, the bridal "toilette was of white satin, had a train at least five yards long, was covered with rare lace and with bouquets and fringes of orange blossom."[11]

The concepts of Worth were rapidly carried to all corners of the globe through illustrations in the fashion magazines. Engravings of Worth garments finished as toilettes with Virot hats, virtually all from the hand of Sandoz, graced the covers of the group of international fashion journals that included *Harper's Bazar* and *The Queen* (fig. 1.30). The numbers rise rapidly from the late 1880s to a peak of thirty-eight issues in 1895. Thereafter, the numbers decrease sharply, so that by 1899 only a handful are found. Over three-quarters of the weekly issues carried at least one, if not two, outfits, sometimes delineated with a reverse aspect. Any accompanying text or editorial comment tended to be minimal; the image was left to make the impression. It might be noted that even when there were remarks, lyricism was not guaranteed. The fashion correspondent for *The Queen*, the British version of *Harper's Bazar*, never rhapsodizes over Worth; her repetitive, chief compliment is some form of "happy," whereas over other couturiers, Pingat in particular, she is much more effusive.

Magazines were laid out in such a manner, or haste, that back and front views of garments were sometimes in separate issues. A portrait of First Lady Mrs. Benjamin Harrison displaced a Worth jacket from the cover of the

1.30 (*Opposite*) Cover of *Harper's Bazar*, Aug. 27, 1892, of Worth "Seaside and Casino Costumes" with Virot hats, as sketched by A. Sandoz and engraved by F. Méaulle. (The smaller, blocked fabric, here in pink damask flowered in green and black and combined with black faille, is found in a Worth walking dress, Pitti Palace, Florence, TA 323–40).

1.31 Worth outfit in bronze velvet, as sketched by Marie de Solar for *L'Art et la mode*, Sept. 27, 1884, and as published in *The Queen*, Oct. 25, 1884, with the offer of a pattern for making up.

October 29, 1891, issue, which included the Sandoz sketch of the back. The full front appeared, as promised, a week later, on November 5. Not recollecting the image or editorial comment of the previous week, readers could well have believed that two different jackets were under discussion: one had a front of "stamped velvet, showing a design of lighter brown leaf sprays sunk in a seal brown velvet ground," the other of "velvet stamped of Havanna brown palms on an otter colored background." Back and sleeves were of "dark brown cloth" in one instance, and of "chestnut-colored cloth" in the other. Both are given gold-colored passementerie and a face-framing beaver collar.

The rapidity with which models were circulated can be traced through an 1884 toilette depicted in the September 27 issue of *L'Art et la mode* (fig. 1.31). Sketched by Marie de Solar, as viewed "chez Worth," it is a robe in bronze velvet with an overskirt draped in panniers terminating in a back pouf. The skirt is in a plain moss silk composed of five deep horizontal pleats, under which pass two other narrower ones. A little cape, fitting the bodice, is arranged with lace that extends over the sleeves. Just one month later, on October 25, 1884, *The Queen* published Solar's sketch as "The Worth Costume," with a "skirt of bronze bengaline trimmed with wide and narrow tucks. The bodice and draperies are bronze plush. The cape is brown lace worked in chenille and mounted on velvet. It terminates with flat bows of velvet ribbon. The gauntlet cuffs correspond." The variations and discrepancies in the two magazines' descriptions may be laid to a combination of translation and editorial prerogatives. Patterns were offered at three shillings, one penny, for the overdress, and one shilling, one penny for the pelerine cape. As to why no skirt pattern was offered, it was a common assumption that a skilled dressmaker would know how to copy an elementary scheme like the simple tucked skirt of this toilette.

In such a manner, Worth designs were distributed not only through models, but also through paper or toile (muslin) patterns. At least two of the many English publications that sold patterns are known to have offered designs based on Worth's, at not an inconsiderable sum. What we do not know today is the procedure for reproduction rights. Did Worth make the patterns available for copying, or did he sell models to pattern publishers for copying? Did the house work on a royalty basis? In the instance of the 1882 polonaise offered by *The Ladies' Treasury*, the pattern purchaser—dressmaker or lady of presumed style—acquired a plain paper pattern, which was stitched, or made up, but untrimmed (patterns often included paper trims), so that fitting adjustments could be made (fig. 1.32). Sometimes a made-up and a flat pattern were offered for the same price. In this way, radical alterations would not destroy the master plan. One size pattern was offered for all.

Another example of 1895 demonstrates the rapid circulation of models. A rendering in *Harper's Bazar* shows a newly modish Louis-XIV style of blue and green shot silk brocaded with large carnations or pinks of many colors and with petticoat and accessories of plain chameleon silk. Fichu drapery encircled the neckline.[12] Supposition is that this popular toilette was made by Worth for one of New York's most prominent importers and dressmakers, Mrs. M. A. Connelly.[13] One week after the rendering appeared, she had in stock Worth Louis-XVI-style coats, with Marie Antoinette fichus to soften the masculine quality; wide revers face the upper sides of the bustline. The "fabric of these coats is something novel, extraordinary in its masses of color like those of illuminated windows of stained glass, ground of taffeta silk, moire and ombré; then encrusted with velvet of very long pile—forming intricate figures and flowers."[14]

When a model was expected to be successful, the fabrics or colors it would be made up in were advertised in the fashion magazines, thus giving us today more insight into the total scale of adaptation possibilities. Young eyes cast in the direction of an 1891 "velvet gown for a young lady [that] is one of Worth's effective adaptations of the First Empire style without its eccentricities" alighted on currant red or found it "could be purchased in éminence purple, Russian blue, dull green, chestnut brown, and black velvet—velvets of a single hue, or of mirror velvet reflecting a contrasting color, or often in wool velvets with dark pile over a lighter background, or else of the still favorite Russian velours with changing surface or cords."[15] Similarly, in 1892, for a mid-winter enveloping long coat, Worth used a very dark blue velvet, with trimming of black fur and gold passementerie (fig. 1.34). Suggested for the copy was black velvet "trimmed with grey or brown fur, sable-, mink- or fox-, and further ornamented with jet [fig. 1.33]."[16]

Members of the Worth family never seem to have voiced concern or disapproval over interpretations of their models, but fashion correspondents did. One writing for *Vogue* in the United States in the spring of 1893 "had the pleasure of seeing a case from Worth opened on the evening of the same day I spent an hour or two on the roof garden of the casino. Thus I had an opportunity to study the same fashions under directly opposite conditions. Worth's gowns and mantles are graceful and refined, intended for the fine porcelain of the feminine world, while at the same casino I saw the same wide skirts, bulging or hanging sleeves, deep cuffs and wide shoulder ruffles, but so badly made, and worn by such coarse and common women, that they seemed to bear no resemblance to Worth's creations."[17]

❧❧❧❧❧

1.32 Worth "Polonaise," for which patterns could be purchased by the public. Advertised in *The Ladies' Treasury*, Feb. 1882.

1.33 House of Worth, *Empire Gown* in velvet, as picture in an A. Sandoz illustration on the cover of *Harper's Bazar*, Nov. 12, 1892.

1.34 This *Harper's Bazar* illustration from 1895 depicts a baroque-strapwork-appliqué jacket nearly identical to midnight blue silk-velvet one with appliqué edged with chenille thread worn by Mrs. Robert Garret (Philadelphia Museum of Art, 74.86.1). The A. Sandoz illustration includes a coordinating skirt.

DESIGNS

1.35 Charles F. Worth. *Evening Ensemble*, composed of two bodices, skirt, and streamered sash, c. 1862. Plain cream silk satin draped with silk tulle; trimmed with faux pearls, crystal beads, and swansdown. Said to have been worn by Mrs. James Flower (née Clara Howard). Museum of the City of New York, Gift of Mr. Pierre Lorillard Barbey, Jr., 77.157.2.

Worth designs of the Opulent Era are memorable for their distinctive fabrics rather than for their lines, as will be seen. In the early years of the house, however, Worth specialized in diffusing both the textile and the cut in tulle-clouded gowns of a spun-sugar, opalescent aura—the confections that waltzed through the Second Empire. The extremely ephemeral nature of silk tulle has distorted our ideas of early Worth gowns from the Worth and Bobergh period. After crushing and crumbling like autumn leaves, the often-brittle tulle net on those gowns has dissolved almost as quickly. Without the diffusing cover of illusion net, the undergowns of slick satin or taffeta have lost their original meaning. An idea of the appearance of the early gowns can be gleaned from paintings. While it is impossible to say for sure the gowns in the Franz Xaver Winterhalter (1805–73) portraits of Princess Tatiana Alexandrovna Youssoupov (1858) and Empress Elizabeth of Austria (1865) are Worth creations, there is strong supporting evidence. Both dresses are characteristically white on white, with an occasional sprinkling of color, as in the embroidered or paillette stars of Elizabeth's toilette. Flowers, ribbons, and other gewgaws in clear pinks, purples, and blues festooned Worth frocks of this period. Such ethereal fashions, which could be whipped up on short order, became the trademark of an era. Of the many pieces so made, only isolated examples, like a multifunctional gown in the Museum of the City of New York (fig. 1.35), survive. This garment is said to be the bridal ensemble

1.36 Charles F. Worth. *Ensemble*, composed of day and evening bodices, skirt, and streamered sash, c. 1864. Plain violet taffeta. The Brooklyn Museum, Designated Purchase Fund, 87.115.

worn by Clara Howard at her marriage to James Flower in 1869. Of cream silk satin, the spreading, crinoline-cage-supported skirt has a very deep, pouffed-over flounce of matching tulle. The skirt and coordinating bodices appear to date from the first half of the decade, and later family members, not being versed in the fashions of the 1850s and 1860s, may have assumed that the garment's color spoke only of a bridal function.[1]

From about 1855 to 1875, many garments were composed as mix-and-match ensembles with not one bodice, but at least two. The richness of the fabric of Clara Howard's bodices, for example, and trim—on one of them, glass-pearl beads and swansdown—would indicate that they were appropriate for evening wear. One was for less formal affairs; it is high necked, with long, coat-shaped sleeves and restrained trims. A streamered belt softens the union of the skirt and the bodice. The other, with scooped neck, pouffed cap sleeve, peplum, and garnishing, was for the most formal of occasions and reveals in its cut the charms admired in the period: sloping shoulders, a tiny waist, and a modestly revealed bosom.

Of all the Worth garments believed to have been fabricated during the house's most active years, from 1860 to 1905, only a fragmentary selection survives. Extant Worth and Bobergh garments dating prior to 1871 are the least numerous, and in several instances bodices survive while their matching skirts were probably cut up to be made over into other garments or girls' dresses. Most of the remaining gowns are of silk taffeta or faille (plain colored or striped) and, like the garment previously described, have two bodices—one for informal events and another for a more glamorous occasion (fig. 1.36). Nothing in their cut, fabric, finish, or trim sets them apart as being

45

1.37 Pencil sketch of a late-1860s day ensemble related to a gown in the collection of the Musée de la Mode et du Costume, Paris (E.12.209–D28). Victoria and Albert Museum, E22394.1957, p. 126.

particularly noteworthy, let alone associated with the revered establishment of Worth. In comparison with Pingat pieces of the same period, workmanship is of a distinctly second order. Several of the design changes attributed to Worth in the late 1860s are to be found in a bottle green taffeta day dress in the collection of the Musée de la Mode et du Costume, Paris (E12.209–D28). The risqué ankle-length skirt no longer bells out over a crinoline but is drawn toward the back and supported by a bustle hoop. Remarkably, the layering once accomplished with tulle is now attempted with fabrics of substance. The five-piece day dress consists of an underskirt, overskirt, front-peplumed bodice, and a spreading, double-tiered, streamered sash, all creating three billowing layers over the hips and terminating in the center back with a punctuation mark—the streamered sash. Around the neck and over the bust goes a matching frilled fichu. The shortened and bustled skirt is ascribed to Worth inventiveness, while the fichu comes from his revivalist urge, which would continue for decades to come. A pencil sketch closely related to this dress is found in the Worth sketchbooks at the Victoria and Albert Museum (Print Department E22394.1957, p. 126, no. 252) (fig. 1.37).

46

1.38 Charles F. Worth. *Princess Afternoon Dress*,
c. 1879. Ticking stripe abutted to dark brown silk
satin matched with polychrome stylized-floral silk
brocade; machine-made lace. Museum of the City of
New York, Gift of Mrs. Fritz Frank, 40.74.2.

In the 1860s, pre-Revolutionary eighteenth-century garments influenced
Worth designs; they may have been considered a reinforcement for the newly
established monarchy of Louis Napoleon. Late in this decade Worth began
his adaptations of seventeenth-century styles, which continued over the
succeeding decades. The influences can be seen not only in design, with back
drapery being supported by a bustle or tonure, but also in weight of fabrics.
Indeed, many Worth garments might be said to be Louisian—Louis XIV,
Louis XV, and Louis XVI. Frequently a single garment will combine the
styles of one period with the fabric of a completely different epoch or
geographical region.

Inspiration for princess-line garments is generally credited to Worth, who
is said to have introduced them in about 1873. Instead of having a cut at or
near the waistline with the bodice and skirt horizontally seamed or left as two
pieces, the princess-line cut was uninterrupted from neck to hemline (fig.
1.38). Garments of this cut probably grew out of two formally "informal"
articles of attire, the wrapper and the tea gown. The objective of a tea gown
was to package formality over a lightly corseted figure, and the unbroken

1.39 Jean-Philippe Worth. *Tea Gown*, c. 1900. Silk-satin striped pink floral brocade, silk chiffon and satin, embroidered net lace. The Brooklyn Museum, Gift of Mrs. C. Oliver Iselin, 61.219.8.

lines afforded by the princess-line cut eventually became almost a trademark of tea gowns (fig. 1.39). Discussion is still held on the genesis of the term "princess" and date of the first models. The most popular claimant is Alexandra, Princess of Wales, whose ideal figure would have looked only more sublime in these near figure-fitting dresses. *The Englishwoman's Domestic Magazine* of February 1875 reveals that the princess dress was firmly enough established by this date to be threatened by an upstart model. Challenging itself, Worth introduced as one of its "modeles de luxe" the "Olga," a gown fitting the figure to perfection, closely molding all its outlines, with folded draping across the front that terminates at the back as a scarf extending over a long and ample train. The "Olga" was introduced after the first of the year, rather than at the commencement of winter, as were the more mundane models. Exhibiting the features of an "Olga" is a dress of cream silk satin, patterned with gold moss rosebuds, with rich trims of silk fringe, cream point d'esprit net, and pale blue silk faille, now in The Metropolitan Museum of Art (69.33.3).

Loose interpretations of late seventeenth-century skirts comprise nearly half of the Worth gowns that survive from the 1870s. Frequently they are mixed with bodices whose sleeves are fully or partially banded horizontally so that, in an early seventeenth-century manner, the filmy fabric of an "undersleeve" may be pulled and pouffed. The First Empire ancestry of high-waisted, low-necked bodices was acknowledged by the appellation Josephine. Two bodices of this cut and date can be identified: one is described as of black chambray gauze with gold-colored stripes made over black silk (see fig. 1.7);[2] and another, a surviving example, is from the Hewitt family, probably having belonged to Mrs. Abram Hewitt, and is of a pale blue novelty-weave gauze flashed with silver-foil stripes (Museum of the City of New York, 30.155.37). The dating of garments is aided by the fact that Worth bodice linings can be related to eras. The earliest are of pearly white China silk, followed in the 1870s with a silk twill-woven stripe in a deep cream tone. These are succeeded by an almost universal application of cream taffeta, which is occasionally replaced by a shade more sympathetic to the coloration of the exterior fabric. Another element that should be borne in mind when one attempts to date Worth garments, and garments in general, is that as clients age, they become more conservative in their taste and revert to fashions of earlier seasons, even though the textile chosen may be of the current mode. Many of the garments from the wardrobe of Mrs. John Quincy Adams of Boston, now in the Museum of Fine Arts, Boston (46.201,.203,.204,.205), would tally with this observation. Her preference was for bodices with elongated and very sharply pointed waists of the early 1880s: these were not totally outmoded by 1890, but neither were they the height of fashion. Coming up on middle age, Mrs. William Alfred Perry also had a preference for such encasing attire. One example from her wardrobe, in The Brooklyn Museum (26.359), sadly now faded, features fabric of wood-hyacinth damask-patterned silk satin made up in an almost medieval cuirasse bodice, where the center front point reaches to the thigh-line. With its inner bodice boning as well as that in the corset, this evening dress must only have evoked comfort when the wearer was standing as if frozen in a statuesque manner.

Wraps—mantles, dolmans, and jackets—are the scarcest Worth articles from the 1870s, and the author has yet to see a firmly attributable 1860s piece. Perhaps it was the feeling that establishments such as Gagelin, Charles Frederick's former employer, were the preeminent creators in this area and competition would be both unnecessary and unprofitable. The earliest labeled outer garment examined by the author is a hip-length jacket of purple velvet flounced at the sides and over the back bustle, with cascades of knife-pleated purple silk faille ribbon, over which a beaded fringe flows (fig. 1.40). Appliqués of cone-shaped glass beads in stylized foliate forms, like those that embellish the back sides, decorate in various permutations outer wraps for

1.40 Charles F. Worth. *Short Jacket*, c. 1872. Royal purple silk velvet and faille; passementerie trims. Union Française des Arts du Costume, Gift of Mme de Galéa, 50.16.5.

1.41 A swaggering sweep of "Grand Manteau" in a totally new form was presented by Hy, as seen at Worth, in *L'Art et la mode*, Aug. 29, 1885.

the coming thirty years. Almost as if heralding the beginning of a new decade, wraps became a wide-ranging and important aspect of the house as the 1880s came in. Visitors to the salon in 1880 would be shown mantles—called Japanese by some and Cossack by others—that were long and loosely fitted at the shoulders, in the manner of a smock: "They are very large and have nothing juvenile about them; but then it is the fashion to try and make the head look young and clothe the figure on cold days in large mantles."[3] Soon a cry arose against these all-enveloping wraps because they concealed handsome and obviously costly dresses (fig. 1.41). Other novelties found in Worth's rooms were mantles said to have been copied with considerable success from sixteenth-century engravings. One was black satin, joined at the back, crossing at the waist, and with two long ends falling to the knees, and ornamented all around with white Venetian point—the lace being so full that around the throat it resembled a swansdown boa. For winter 1881 Worth made a severely elegant "Etole," or stole-shaped mantle, which was based, according to *The Queen*, on "the sleeveless garment worn by priests in church."[4] The somber black embossed, or ciselé, velvet-face fabric for this wrap was relieved by vivid ombré linings in bright pinks shaded to red, lemon to amber, lapis to sky blue, and alga green to apple green.

In a rare practical stroke, the house "invented" in 1881 an inner lining to cut bitter cold. Sleeveless, quilted eiderdown-filled *casaquins* were vestlike garments to be worn under mantles or wraps of silk or satin that were lined only with a thinner silk. When one was paying a visit, it was only necessary to remove the outer wrap, revealing a brocaded underwrap.[5]

Because of the diversity of design in the period of the late 1870s to mid-1880s, there are very few points in common held by the garments examined by the author. All but one of the dresses have low-cut necks and the less formal have elongated square necks. Descriptions of two court dresses from the Worth workrooms of 1880–81 reveal unity only in coloration. The American Lillie (Moulton) de Hegermann-Lindencrone, by now wife of a Danish diplomat, wrote from Rome of her first official appearance at the Italian court at Quirinal. This "splendid ceremony took place at two o'clock in the afternoon, a rather trying time to be décolleté and look your best, even in a quite lovely white brocade gown with the tulle front all embroidered with iridescent beads and pearls. The manteau de court—my first court train—is of white satin trimmed with valenciennes lace and ruches of chiffon. I wore my diamond tiara, my pearls on my neck and everything I owned in the way of jewelry pinned on me somewhere."[6] The fashion observer for *The Queen* found a court dress—destined, she believed, for London—which came preglittered: "The petticoat was white satin and the train white and silver damask. Down the side were sprays of white hyacinths, the stalks being powdered with silver, the low bodice was pointed at the waist, and the satin plastron, as well as the skirt, were embroidered with silver, on the bodice were three white bows in the form of geranium flowers."[7]

The garments from the all-white- or all-black-label period (see p. 27),[8] from about 1882 to about 1886, began to herald several design elements that would become important features (pls. 4, 6). Aside from the stripping away of layered fabrics and outrageous applications of trims, design reference and cut were notable. Features with clearly defined historical precedents were introduced into ordinary day wear. The sleeve cap was raised and enlarged: the leg-of-mutton, or gigot, sleeves of the 1830s would rise to their fully exaggerated potential in 1894.

In 1885–86 the house intensified its development of designs based on historical prototypes other than those of the eighteenth century. Previously, such prototypes had figured prominently only in designs for fancy-dress costume balls, which had grown in popularity since being started by Queen Victoria in the 1840s, and which remained stylish into the new century. For fancy-dress functions, lavish imitation was called for; it was no fun if nobody recognized from the costume the role that was being played.

Woven white on white, gold on black – narrow ribbon
20th century, found additionally in accessories

In general, as the 1880s closed (fig. 1.42), a verticality of garment design had superseded the horizontal pastiches of trim from the first half of the decade, and fabrics of monumental design were increasingly becoming a house signature. In among the moss and other roses, one finds staggeringly lifelike full-blown parrot tulips (pl. 8), peas in stripped-open pods (Museum of Fine Arts, Boston, 46.204), and other realistic interpretations. Special note should be made of two quite different dresses, but each incorporating a house design element reminiscent of Castiglione's celestial motifs (pl. 7). The first is a remarkably restrained day dress enhanced only with a touch of lace, dated to about 1886 and belonging to Sarah Evans Lippincott (fig. 1.43). The primary fabric strikes the viewer as the heavens, observed through a telescope of great power. The blue-black, changeable to olive green, silk taffeta ground is liberally sprinkled with white constellation-like features. Counterbalancing the simplicity of this work is perhaps one of the house's most dazzlingly brilliant creations (fig. 1.45). As a young matron, Mrs. Caroline Schermerhorn Astor Wilson stunned fellow guests with an evening dress whose entire skirt front panel was appliquéd and embroidered in gold and silver bugle beads with a sunburst radiating through small cumulus clouds. The burst is set against white satin and framed by a star-and-cloud beaded border and aqua-tinted satin. Touches of layered rainbow-hued pink, blue, and yellow silk chiffons, including Henri II puffs on the hips, complete this ethereal gown fashioned between 1887 and 1890.

By the end of the 1880s, most of the decorative emphasis of the skirt except for any fabric patterning had been brought to the center front, with trains sweeping away in unembellished splendor. Once again, as earlier in the decade, the bustle was dropping gradually, in what would be a final recessional. The latent gore, which had been a part of Worth's modified eighteenth-century front tablier design for so long, would in the 1890s become a structural rather than decorative device in skirt construction: the basic pattern for many skirts of the nineties simply called for six straight breadths of fabric, which could be draped and trimmed according to whim. Charles Frederick Worth and a few holdover couturiers from the 1860s, like Laferrière and Felix, understood the interrelationship of fabric, cut, and construction and why, with increasingly stout figures and heavy fabrics, it was necessary to cut bulk from the waist, as it had been in the 1860s, when gored skirts had been previously fashionable. An early mention of the gored skirt is made in 1890. ''The gored skirt is Worth's scheme of doing away with fullness at the top of back breadths, yet having them so broad at the foot that they spread out roundly as they lie on the floor . . . . [fig. 1.44]''[9]

In the sort of romantic association eagerly swallowed by the public, *Harper's Bazar* credited Queen Victoria with the reappearance of gored skirts in the 1890s, relating that the ''revival began in London and is said to owe its

1.42 (*Opposite*) A bevy of Worth evening toilettes as depicted in *L'Illustration*, c. 1890.

1.43 Charles F. Worth. *Day Dress*, c. 1886. Midnight blue changeable to dark olive brocade silk with tiny starlike white dots and olive silk faille; machine-made lace. Worn by Sarah Evans Lippincott. Cincinnati Art Museum, Gift of Mr. and Mrs. Oliver Lippincott Bailey, 1986.1071.

1.44 Worth attire for promenading in town, 1894.

1.45 (*Opposite*) Charles F. and/or Jean-Philippe Worth. *Ball Toilette*, c. 1890. Pastel shades of silk satin and chiffon; embroidered with shimmering sunburst through cumulus clouds. Worn by Caroline Schermerhorn Astor Wilson. The Metropolitan Museum of Art, Gift of Orme and R. Thornton Wilson in memory of their mother, Caroline Schermerhorn Astor Wilson, 49.3.28.

origins to the discovery by Sir Henry Ponsonby, the Queen's secretary, of a collection of dolls that were dressed by the Queen when she was the little Duchess of Kent. The gowns of that period [the 1830s] were well reproduced in those outfits by the painstaking child, and the dressmakers, appreciating the find, copied them. French couturiers in search of novelty soon seized on these London models."[10]

Fashion journals of the late 1880s and early 1890s proclaim a return to Empire lines. It is fortunate that we have this documentation, for, with one or two exceptions, one would never recognize any relationship between the structured, waisted, bustled, heavy-fabricated pieces of the fin de siècle and the flimsy, clinging, high-waisted, soft-fabricated pieces of nearly a century earlier.

Three almost identical true Empire-inspired gowns exist. Two from the collection of The Brooklyn Museum originally belonged to a member of the Roebling family (pl. 9) and Mrs. Frederick Prince (67.110.103), while a third

1.46 Charles F. and/or Jean Philippe Worth. *Empire Style Evening Frock*, c. 1892. Gray silk satin and fuchsia velvet; bead and sequin embroidery, handmade lace. Worn by Mrs. Augustus Newland Eddy (née Abbie Louise Spencer). Chicago Historical Society, Gift of Mr. Albert J. Beveridge III, 1976.270.7.

1.47 Another Worth interpretation of eighteenth-century dress adapted to the bustle-and-drape mode of the 1880s. Made in soft olive wool with beaver trim. From *Harper's Bazar*, March 27, 1886.

is in the Musée de la Mode et du Costume, Paris (73.14.2). All have the same trimmings, gilt spangles and glass beads, but the fabric varies: one is a wool and silk ottoman, the second a silk rep, and the third a satin. At the Chicago Historical Society is yet another variation, this time trained, and with more elaborate hemline embroidery (fig. 1.46). According to family tradition, Mrs. Augustus Newland Eddy—for whom the gown of gray satin decorated with fuchsia velvet and with silver sequins and beads was made—thought it was based on Jacques-Louis David's (1745–1825) rendering of Empress Josephine at the coronation of Napoleon I.

To begin the final decade of the century, high round waists and flaring capes with matching high flaring collars were said to have been inspired by Empress Josephine and her times; and credit for the figure eight's displacement of the *V* and inverted *V* went to the sixteenth and seventeenth centuries rather than to the very momentarily inelegant eighteenth century. In about 1891 square necklines, like those seen in the portraits of Tudor royalty such as Elizabeth I and Anne of Cleves, the fourth wife of Henry VIII, came into vogue. Inspiration, according to Jean-Philippe, was derived from the works of artists such as Hans Holbein, whose portrait of the unappealing Anne is one of his major works. Early in the nineties comes mention of a "Louis Quatorze" coat to a visiting ensemble that was to change

1.48 Jean-Philippe Worth. *Promenade Suit*, c. 1892. Deep green silk velvet; embroidered in metallic threads in concert with the eighteenth-century style of the suit. Worn by Anne Cheney of the Cheney Mill family. Wadsworth Atheneum, Hartford, Gift of Frank D. Cheney, 1957.47.

little over the decade, as can be seen in two variants later owned by the Hewitt sisters, originally made as part of a magnificent deep dark green velvet metallic-thread-embroidered suit belonging to Anne Cheney (fig. 1.48).[11] These were "encrusted with appliqué embroidery opening on a white satin vest with silver buttons and a lace jabot. The full . . . sleeves have deep embroidered cuffs, with a black watered ribbon bow (set inside each arm) [pl. 17]."[12] Never far removed from the eighteenth century, the house created a rather mannishly severe tailored gown (fig. 1.47), highlighted with a strange combination of design elements from the past for a "stately gown with princess back and coat front suitable for reception and carriage toilette. [It is a] combination of one of the 'fin de siècle' brocades with peau de soie of the same color richly embroidered. A feather pattern brocade—all black and in stripes, opens on an embroidered peau de soie vest with a bodice front deep frill."[13] The color selection highlighted in an engraved watercolored version (fig. 1.49) hardly dilutes the masculine impression—iron gray, dark gray, and white—and would seem to make the sale of this dress, advertised to be copied as a wedding gown, difficult.

Although most surviving Worth garments date from the years between 1890 and about 1905, it has proved impossible, with very few exceptions, to correlate extant garments to photographs and/or engravings or to written

1.49 A pastiche of patterns is found in Worth's "Reception" or "Carriage" tailor-gown cut inspired by eighteenth-century men's suits, with princess back and coat fronts. The muddle continues in the fin de siècle feather-patterned striped brocade. Sketched by A. Sandoz and published as the cover of *Harper's Bazar*, Oct. 10, 1891.

1.50 Charles F. and/or Jean-Philippe Worth. *Reception Dress*, 1897. Vermiculate silk damask in white and steel gray; handmade tape lace, peach silk faille. Worn by Mrs. Calvin Brice. Museum of the City of New York, Anonymous Gift, 42.146.20.

1.51 (*Above right*) *Harper's Bazar* and related publications in late 1893 to early 1894 included this Sandoz sketch of one of the most perennially popular Worth designs, a reception dress in the seventeenth-century manner. Loosely fitted, it was perfect for large ladies.

1.52 The actress Emma Eames, photographed in her version of the Worth 1894 reception dress.

descriptions. A near match comes with the tea gown (fig. 1.50) that belonged, as is clear from its generous proportions, to Mrs. Calvin Brice—not to one of her daughters, whose Worths also survive. Combining historical elements, but predominantly of Louis XIII style, with a later "Watteau" pleated back, the gown has a broad collar of real tape lace over full, but enlarged, seventeenth-century sleeves. Decorative self material and corded points "lash" the falling overskirt to the concealed yoke. The fabric of the outer gown is steel gray silk damask worked with a vermiculate motif in white; this rests atop a cream silk-satin false petticoat. Another version (pl. 15) was worn and altered by a Hewitt, but the rows of silvery blue peacock feathers of the fabric turn this variant into as much an Aesthetic Movement robe as a historical derivative. Emma Eames, the operatic singer, had another version, which, regrettably, has survived only in photographic form (fig. 1.52). The published gown graces the cover of the February 3, 1894, issue of *Harper's Bazar* (fig. 1.51), which additionally includes a two-thirds back profile. Interrelationships of garments and fabrics can be deduced from another related garment: it is readily apparent, from visuals, how the neckline falls on an opera mantle of 1883 (fig. 1.53) might have influenced the "Watteau" back, or how the fabric used to illustrate this mantle might have persuaded the Hewitts of its suitability in a tea gown. In the Hewitt gown a bright, light

58

blue satin serves as the petticoat and, in contrast to the Brice example, faces the openings of the outer sleeve seam. The Hewitt gown is not identified with an order number, whereas the Brice one is, leading to the conclusion that the Brice example was made up at a later date, when this system of identification and business management was more firmly entrenched.

In other instances of correlating extant garments with visuals, two nearly identical versions of a gown are known and can be related to a photographed model. The photographed garment is no. 502, year 1902–3, of the house design albums.[14] The dress of chiné, or warp-printed, silk taffeta is printed in a bowed, swagged, floral garland combined with machine-made lace. One version of this rustling Belle Epoque fantasy is held by the Museum of Fine Arts, Boston (no. 62252, year 1903), and the second version was previously in the private collection of the late J. Herbert Callister (fig. 1.59), former Curator of Costumes at the Wadsworth Atheneum, Hartford. Shown at The Brooklyn Museum in 1962, it was sold at auction, and its present whereabouts are unknown.

In a particularly intriguing case, a garment can be related to a visual as well as to an actual historical prototype. On the cover of the April 13, 1895, issue of *Harper's Bazar* (fig. 1.56), we find a sketch of a "spring cape" by Adolf Sandoz,[15] described in the magazine as follows: "Colored velvet [is] chosen for richest wraps of the spring and will be worn at Newport for afternoon driving throughout the summer. Dark garnet velvet lined with cream-white satin effectively wrought with soutache of matte silver outline stripes wide border. Hoodlike a golf cape and long parrot points, both finished with tassels of garnet silk and silver thread. Front of cape turned back in revers that display cream satin of the lining." A version of this medieval-looking cape originally worn by Mrs. C. Oliver Iselin of Providence, Rhode Island, is to be found in dark olive green silk velvet at The Brooklyn Museum (fig. 1.57). Worth's inspiration for this wrap is a cape, now in the Germanisches National Museum of Nuremberg (fig. 1.55), that relates to men's wraps of Spanish origin dating between 1570 and 1580.[16] The prototype cape is short, semicircular, of an ivory twill, heavily milled woven woolen cloth embroidered in dark brown (probably originally black). The hood is embellished with brown woolen tufts. It was purchased by the Nuremberg Museum in 1903, and speculations as to its peregrinations between at least late 1894 to early 1895, when the Worth wrap first must have been made, and 1903, when it entered the Nuremberg collection, are numerous. Did Worth acquire the cape for copying? Did a Parisian antiquarian or dealer in secondhand clothes make it available for adaptation? Was it sold out of France directly into Germany? Clearly it was recognized as an important piece at the time and shortly thereafter, as it is pictured in editions of Emma von Sichart and Carl Köhler's classic German book on historic costume, *Praktische Kostüm Kunde*.

1.53 Opera mantle fashioned from the peacock-feather-eye fabric as utilized in the Hewitt gown (pl. 15).

1.54 Charles F. and/or Jean-Philippe Worth. *Reception Dress*, c. 1895. Strapwork-patterned cream silk velvet; Battenburg tape lace. Museum of the City of New York, Gift of Mrs. Moorehead C. Kennedy, 85.49.

1.55 (*Above*) *Man's Riding Cape*, Spanish, c. 1580, used by the House of Worth in fashioning an 1895 woman's cape. Germanisches Nationalmuseum, Nuremberg.

1.56 (*Above right*) Sandoz rendering of the late Renaissance Spanish man's riding cape, as interpreted by the House of Worth. Published as the cover of *Harper's Bazar*, April 13, 1895.

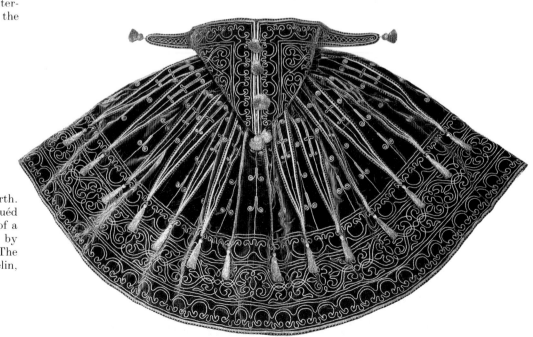

1.57 Charles F. and/or Jean-Philippe Worth. *Spring Cape*, 1895. Dark olive silk velvet; appliquéd metallic silver soutache braid. A direct copy of a man's sixteenth-century Spanish cape. Worn by Mrs. C. Oliver Iselin (née Hope Goddard). The Brooklyn Museum, Gift of Mrs. C. Oliver Iselin, 61.219.4.

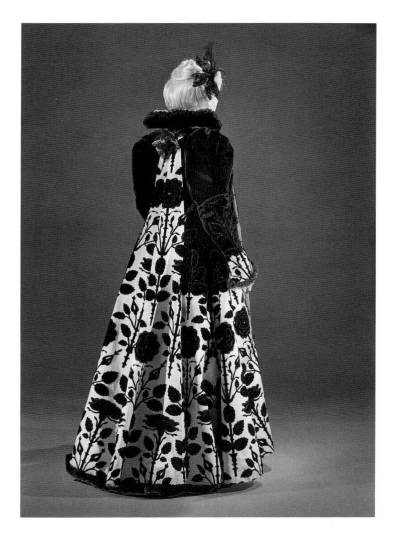

1.58 Jean-Philippe Worth. *Opera Coat*, c. 1900. Black and white voided velvet patterned with a Tudor rose motif; black velvet, white silk chiffon and black Chantilly lace. Fashioned into a sixteenth-century-inspired wrap. The Brooklyn Museum, Gift of Mrs. William E. Griswold, 41.910.

1.59 (*Below left*) Two examples of this 1902–3 warp-printed silk taffeta dress are known to have survived. The model is directly traceable through the Worth photographic archives as model no. 502. Collection of the late J. Herbert Callister.

1.60 (*Below*) A loosely interpreted seventeenth-century-style dress. Museum of the City of New York, Gift of Mrs C. Lorillard Spencer, 40.401.1.

1.61 Worth's 1894 historical perspective of the fin de siècle of the previous century. The full, rounded, unbroken bust was to be the coming feature as yet another century turned.

It is surmised that Jean-Philippe Worth had a strong, if not greater, affinity for past modes than his father, since historical interpretation continued in Worth designs after Charles Frederick's death (fig. 1.58). The Worth/Paquin Archives at the Victoria and Albert Museum give us some idea of the more widely distributed visual references utilized by the firm (fig. 1.60). At the designers' call were late eighteenth-century sketches and fashion plates from *Gallerie des modes*, among others, as well as later publications (fig. 1.61). Paintings in major collections are said to have provided inspiration. Artists the family looked to included, along with those already mentioned, Titian, Rembrandt, and, during Charles Frederick's brief days in London when visits were made to the National Gallery, Sir Joshua Reynolds. Credit for garments other than fancy-dress toilettes is given to Anthony van Dyck, Thomas Gainsborough, and two mid-eighteenth-century French artists, Nicolas de Largillière (1656–1746) and Jean-Marc Nattier (1685–1766).[17] Sadly, no direct correlation has been established between any specific work of art and a Worth garment, excluding fancy dress. And surely the only inspirations Nattier offered were pastel silks, and lavish floral festoons more flamboyant than even the "artiste" Worth dared to deploy.

Published and unpublished references occur, however. One, and it is ambiguous at that, is made to an artist in conjunction with a garment: Worth's short Rembrandt red velvet mantle with a large collar faced with rose satin and front of Chantilly lace, with trimmings of a broad galoon of jet scattered with rubies.[18] As no rendering confirms the intended association, reasonable questions arise: was the model cape taken from a Rembrandt or a Rembrandt red, or is the name just applied to a Worth garment as promotional hyperbole?

Speculation might also be offered on the authorship of the garment Caroline (Mrs. William B.) Astor (fig. 1.62) is attired in for her full-length portrait by Charles-Emile-Auguste Carolus-Duran (1838–1917). Sober but exceedingly rich in materials, it would seem to be a combination of the gowns worn by several of van Dyck's sitters: Beatrice de Cusance, princess of Cantecroix, provides the black coloration and the overall appearance, while her contemporary the duchess of Lorraine offers her lace collar, stomacher, and slightly opened center skirt front revealing a patterned underskirt. The shape, but not the construction, of the sleeves may have been inspired by those in a full-length portrait of an unknown woman. The cuffs of this woman's toilette have been appropriated, too.[19]

Two 1902–3 garments in the Chicago Historical Society (1976.270.9, 1976.270.10) by tradition are linked to portraits of Mme Sophie and Mme Henriette de Bourbon Conte by Jean-Marc Nattier, but a review of his oeuvre has failed to establish the relationship. These garments were made for mother and daughter, Mrs. Augustus Newland Eddy (née Abbie Louise Spencer) and

1.62 The famous Mrs Astor (née Caroline Webster Schermerhorn) in her imposing portrait of 1890 by Charles-Emile-Auguste Carolus-Duran (1838–1917). Her seventeenth-century-style gown is thought to be a Worth. The Metropolitan Museum of Art, Gift of R. Thornton Wilson and Orme Wilson, 49.4.

Mrs. Albert J. Beveridge (née Catherine Eddy). Mrs. Eddy's gown of blue taffeta, trimmed with lace, tulle, gold-thread embroidery, and blue plush had floral-garland trim of silk flowers especially made by Camille Marchais. Sweetly ingenue, her daughter's dress is of a floral- and vine-figured pink taffeta trimmed with blonde lace, a self-material floral garland faced with cloth of gold, and white tulle.[20]

The styles of Louis XIII and Revolutionary France cast their spell on the final decade of the nineteenth century. Scattered references continued to be made also to the styles associated with Mme Pompadour, while some clients

1.63 A design feature espoused by Worth in the early 1890s was the placement of functional metal hooks and eyes as decorative features, as seen on the right-hand figure of this *Harper's Bazar* cover of June 11, 1892.

1.64 Close inspection reveals that the "sequins" trimming a gray-blue silk-velvet jacket dated c.1897 and in the eighteenth-century style are actually silver-dust-flocked cardboard discs. The Brooklyn Museum, Gift of the Princess Viggo in accordance with the wishes of the Misses Hewitt, 31.62.

like Princess Charlotte de la Tremoille would expect to find in their trousseaux neck-ruffed robes à la Henri II (fig. 1.65).

Even as Worth drew inspiration from portraits of the past, some of his clients sat for portraits wearing attire designed by the house. Carolus-Duran might be considered the co-official portraitist of Worth clients along with Winterhalter. The sitters did not always wear Worth designs, but some clients apparently did purchase a garment with an eye to sitting for a portrait in such regalia. Advice was offered on what translated best on canvas: "Peau de soie, a rich silk as smooth as the softest human skin is used. This is a closely twilled fabric much like satin but without the hard luster of satin to which artists object."[21]

Some of the dressmaking techniques employed by Worth over the years are as interesting as the garments or fabrics themselves (figs. 1.63, 1.64). The senior Worth has been credited with achieving a better fit in his early designs. Further enhancing the idealized, well-rounded, feminine figure acquired through the artifice of corset and crinoline, he placed the warp threads of the fabric weave in the direction taken by the principal movements of the body. Thus we initially find a fanning of the warp over the upper torso with the vertical format placed at center front and back, and the bias directed to the mid-side regions. By the second half of the 1860s this construction detail becomes less prominent.

As significant as Worth's improvement of fit was his espousal of mix-and-match garment parts. While early nineteenth-century fashion illustrators would interchange bodices, skirts, and headwear in order to create a "new" fashion, Worth went even further. He would begin with a basic garment shape, such as an overskirt, then add a flounce, flower, frill, or any combination of them, and—presto—he would have a unique skirt, just what was needed to supply the rapacious demands of his ladies. The genius of mixing and matching of parts is readily apparent in the house sketch archives now lodged at the Victoria and Albert Museum, wherein multitudes of inspirations for skirts from the 1860s and early 1870s exist.[22] For the bodices, high necks could be slashed for décolletage, long coat sleeves could be replaced with short caps or long, flowing pseudo-medieval ones. The interchangeable parts and trims provided almost ceaseless variety. Such an assembly-line approach to dressmaking probably drove Worth to adopt his personal artistic demeanor: it was essential for him to be perceived as a creative genius, not a mechanic turning out die-cut apparel.

Many of the mundane but all-important internal workings of the house still have not been revealed. As early as the 1860s, Worth and Bobergh, perhaps in the long-established tradition of couture, bought model sketches from outside designers. A series of watercolored sketches in the Worth/Paquin

LE MARIAGE DE LA PRINCESSE CHARLES DE LA TRÉMOILLE

1.65   The wedding trousseau of Princess Charles de la Tremoille, including a bridal and Henri-II-style gown from Worth. Sketched by Hy for *L'Art et la mode*, Oct. 24, 1885.

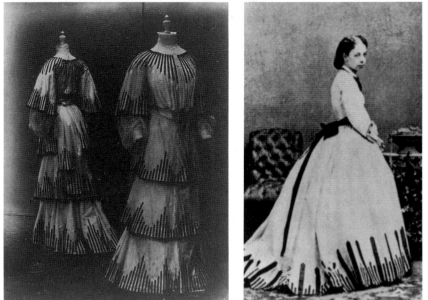

1.66 Design concept for an evening dress of c. 1865 by Ch. Pillate, who is believed to have executed model sketches on speculation for Worth. Private collection.

1.67 (*Above right*) Jean-Philippe Worth's adaptation of an early design favored by his father. Dated 1903; model no. 1200. Victoria and Albert Museum.

1.68 (*Above, far right*) Princess von Metternich in a black and white Worth creation made c. 1865.

1.69 (*Below*) Watercolored house sketch for a summer walking outfit in blue with black trim, c. 1865. Victoria and Albert Museum, E22208–1957/96D10.

1.70 (*Below right*) Watercolor by Laure Noël (1827–1878) for publication as a fashion illustration, c. 1855. The vertical stepped motif at the hemlines of the right-hand figure is to become a House of Worth trademark motif. Sotheby's, London.

1.71 (*Below, far right*) A fashionable Frenchwoman in a slightly later adaptation of Worth's gown for princess von Metternich.

Archives at the Victoria and Albert have been cut out from the works of a designer whose signature could be confused with that of Ch(arles) Worth. Rather, these are from the hand of Ch. Pillate (fig. 1.66), a designer who is known to have sold model sketches to Alexandre Ghys, a widely advertised French dressmaker of the 1860s and 1870s.[23] Questions about the possible interchange are raised: Did Worth purchase sketches with the idea of making up or adapting them as garments? Was Pillate ever on staff at Worth as a house designer? Did the house acquire these sketches later as revival references? Another artist whose published sketches appear in the archives is Gustave Janet (b. 1829), whose work was published in *La Mode Artistique*, *Mode Illustré*, and *Revue de la mode*.[24]

Another possible instance of in-house imitative impulse occurred in 1903, when the house issued an adaptation of one of its founder's earliest garments (fig. 1.67). Through a photograph of about 1865, the design is best associated with princess von Metternich (fig. 1.68). A sketch for the princess's light-and-dark dress along with its waist-length cape is to be found in the Worth model sketch archives, in blue with black trim.[25] This may not (fig. 1.69) have been the first version, however, for fashion illustrator Laure Noël (1827–78)

1.72   A bright pink-topped outfit for adventures in town, 1894.

sketched a four-flounced skirted evening dress with vertical tripart striping bordering each flounce (fig. 1.70) in about 1855. A variation of Metternich's dress is worn by an elegant Frenchwoman in a photograph of 1867 (fig. 1.71). Alterations can be noted in the diminution of scale and authority of the hemline decoration, with the stripes now regimented in width and length, and the scallops shrunken. When the design was revived in 1903 (fig. 1.67), only the decoration harked back to the princess's version, although the double-flounced skirt may well have had its genesis in the initial model of the mid-1850s, despite the fact that in the last years of the century Jean-Philippe had expressed the view that the modern woman's love for athletics, though deplorable from his aesthetic point of view, had made any revival of the crinoline impossible.[26]

Further insight into the house's internal workings is gained from several remarks made in the American press during the 1890s concerning the delinquency with which Worth would provide new season fashions. Had he not yet decided the momentous question of winter fashions? He would reveal nothing and positively refused "to send over a case of winter gowns and mantles even to his best customers before the middle of October. The nearly unthinkable solutions were either to make our own fashions or to look shabby for the next two months."[27] In London the same concern was expressed. Women waited anxiously to be assured of the authentic 1894 fashions, about which so many contradictory rumors floated. So conflicting were the signals that even the above-cited article's author was confused, proclaiming eighteenth-century ringlets would go with Empire gowns and accessories.

67

1.73, 1.74 Worth wrap with swags of jet beads, said to have been inspired by "old Egyptian costumes" sketched by A. Sandoz and published on the cover of *Harper's Bazar*, March 4, 1893; May Routh's 1977 interpretation as an evening dress, styled c. 1902, for Ann-Margret as Lady Flavia in *The Last Remake of Beau Geste*. Los Angeles County Museum of Art, Gift of May Routh 1987, M86.406.8.

But would the new modes be "modelled on the whims and fancies of dramatic Paris, in collusion with Messrs. Worth, Pacquin [sic] and Doucet, the reigning artists du modes of gay Lutetia."?[28] This unresolved state had actually begun in late spring, when an American had revealed that

> she had tried in vain to induce Worth, Pingat or any other leading cloak or dress maker to take her orders and measures for next winter.
>
> It was in vain that she urged her indifference to being absolutely in the height of the fashion, her preference for styles a little passé, and her desire to get a whole year's outfit off her mind while she was on the spot and could superintend the choosing of colors and material. She was assured that so great a change would take place . . . before November that anything purchased now would be absolutely Gothic by that time. "You will see with your eyes," said the venerable Worth . . . "that the change will be enormous, and what I make for you now you would throw to the dogs before Christmas."[29]

To conclude this discussion of Worth's designs, it is appropriate to note that just as Worth had reinterpreted the garments of the past, so were the house's clothes themselves adapted. In 1976 the English costume designer May Routh revamped a "Worth cloak seen in the Louvre" (figs. 1.73, 1.74). This coat appeared on the cover of *Harper's Bazar* on March 4, 1893.[30] A long coat with Persian lamb revers and long full sleeves, it has as a memorable feature—multitudinous rows of jet-bead fringe caught in deep festoons with a central oval bustline jet cabochon, from which cascade many more fringes. Removing the revers and sleeves and radically diminishing the beaded festoons, Routh came up with a Belle Epoque evening "toilette" for Ann-Margret as she played Lady Flavia Geste in the film *The Last Remake of Beau Geste* (1977).

❦❧ ❦❧ ❦❧ ❦❧

TEXTILES, TRIMS, AND TECHNIQUES

Charles Frederick Worth made it a principle to encourage the various industries related to the dressmaking trades in France in response to the ongoing support he received from them. The greatest benefactors were to be the textile mills of Lyon. Worth and his heirs sought to bring renewed and continuing prosperity to this city long famed for its fine textile commodities. Upon the death of Charles Frederick, one of the first actions of the Worth sons was to send a substantial order for the most magnificent materials known to the silk manufacturers of Lyon, affirming that the house would carry on its tradition of employing only the best. For the next twenty years, up to World War I, singular fabrics were one of the glories of Maison Worth. Then the devastation of the War spread, striking the centuries-old mills, cutting down uniquely qualified weavers whose skills could never be duplicated by machines. The majority of fin de siècle Worth garments are most readily recognized from their fabric rather than their design (figs. 1.75, 1.76). The years have not been kind to many of the materials, however. From the sampling of Worth garments inspected for this project, approximately ninety percent were of a pure-silk or silk-mixture fabric. Nearly all the silk tulles have dissolved owing to sizing applications, and other chemical treatments applied to change the hand, or feel, of later silks have meant an early demise for many exceptional works of woven art. Such has been the unfortunate fate met by many satins and taffetas from the turn of this century that have shattered and crumbled into oblivion. In 1882, a date that from today's point of view provided relatively stable silk goods, we read that "all French silks and satins in France, that are intended for foreign markets, are made with the express purpose of cutting and greasing soon. . . . French silk cuts and greases at the first wear, unless a great price is paid for it, and even then cannot be depended upon."[1] The great price just referred to was twelve francs a meter, a price below which the "celebrated Bonnet" would not guarantee any silk. Bonnet, a renowned Lyonnaise silk manufacturer, who by 1894 was exhibiting as Les Petits-Fils de C. F. Bonnet & Cie, was one of the manufacturers weaving for Worth.

Jean-Philippe claims that the first textile woven especially for the house was to have been based on the golden cloak draping Queen Elizabeth I in the "Rainbow" portrait of about 1600 attributed to Marcus Gheeraerts the Younger, a favorite picture from père Worth's youth. The queen's mantle is adorned with alternating centered rows of eyes and ears; through some oversight, however, the first run of fabric made for Worth was embellished only with eyes. Some ten or fifteen years later, Jean-Philippe states, the fabric was reissued with the corrective addition of the ears. The pattern was constructed in "a new material, 'velours au sabare,' of the sort that was woven under Louis XVI, but not so fine in quality."[2]

One of the little-explored aspects of the house is its unique selection of fabrics, especially yard goods. Certain motifs almost became house hallmarks but, by their very nature, are also part of the public-domain design vocabulary (pls. 7, 20). Among the more commonly repeated motifs are stripes, feathers, wheat, stars, butterflies (fig. 1.77), carnations, irises, tulips (fig. 1.78), chestnut and oak leaves, scallops and scales, and bowers of roses. It is recognized that the house issued directives for the configuration of certain

69

patterns, but just what percentage of their materials they designed themselves is not known. Nor has it been revealed who they employed to do the renderings.

Extant garments of the early days, up through the fall of the Second Empire, indicate that nothing really separated Worth fabrics at that time from those utilized by a wide spectrum of dressmakers. The materials tended to be undistinguished and indistinguishable plain-colored taffetas and failles. Tour de force trimmings on gowns that were once tulle-clouded must have been, as much as anything, the magnet for clients, since fabrics and cut are fundamental.

Around 1870 scallops—van Dyck or sawtooth or chevron points (pl. 1)— and stripes made an appearance. With the exception of one or two designs, diminutive motifs prevailed. There was a linear and geometrical emphasis in the fabric design, with stripe variations predominating. One example is a delicate blocked stripe Egyptian-revival motif (pl. 3). While the motif is diminutive, by both Egyptian and Worth standards, the wearer was not. In other instances, variants of acanthus leaves encircling a "column" were deployed in silk damask and applied as embroidery on velvet (The Brooklyn Museum, 29.941.23).

1.75, 1.76 (*Opposite and above*) Mrs. Calvin Stewart Brice, wife of a U.S. senator from Lima, Ohio, and a society matron of considerable presence, counted among her Worths an evening ensemble of coordinating silk velvets—magenta and white—in a stylized Turkish-inspired palmette motif. The outfit consists of gown and sleeveless mantle. The identical patterned fabric was chosen by Jean-Philippe Worth when he assumed the dress of Capulet in 1898. (Dress, Museum of the City of New York, Anonymous Gift, 42.146.)

1.77 The seated figure is gowned in white damask powdered with very small butterflies. The very same fabric is found today in two evening dresses— one cream, the other copper—and in a sober black wrap. A. Sandoz for *Harper's Bazar*, Sept. 17, 1892.

The Queen reported in the fall of 1881 that the announcement that M. Worth intended using English woolen materials for outdoor costumes was an error, and the master wished to deny such a report for, as the world was aware, the house made toilettes of rich stuffs and left the woolens to specialists such as his compatriot Charles Creed, whose business was just down the street cornering on the place de l'Opéra. Worth's reasoning for this stance seems simple enough: his house was essentially French and he had no desire to change the path in which he won his fame. Nevertheless, in 1880 he had encouraged French manufacturers of woolen stuffs to perfect their product so that their materials might rival those of the British Isles, and in 1881 many Worth wraps were turned out in nearly unadorned woolen cloths. Two redingotes, Worth's protest against a detested bunched-up pannier at the back, appear in back-to-back issues of *The Ladies' Treasury* in 1882. The illustrated example could be made up from a plain pattern available for two shillings, two pence. It is of plain very blue woolen cloth, trimmed with gold braid and gold "Brandenbourgs." The back has an insert of pleated blue silk.

In the early 1880s the fabrics of choice were, for the most part, plain silks—velvets, satin moirés, poplins, and reps, with very few striped materials, which were leftovers from the 1870s and had become unmodishly common by 1881. Silk tulle—that fabric that floated Worth to fame during the Second Empire—returned, to be draped over satin and caught with a profusion of flowers (pl. 2). "Never do I remember such a quantity of floral adornments as are worn at present," wrote an observer.[3] Worth was now also dressing the coming-of-age daughters of his earliest clients, and predictably, the very young conspired to look older and the aging wished to recapture their youth.

A fashion correspondent wrote in 1881: "Birds, I rejoice to say, have disappeared and flowers have resumed their prestige."[4] Birds may have temporarily flown from frocks, but beaks and beady eyes were still nestled among the plumage that dressed headwear, tippets, and muffs. Back the birds would flit during the 1882 season, for four or five dark blue birds nested amid the tulle of a ball dress commissioned by Mme de Villeneuve: "The adult size birds flocked to the skirt while around the neck roosted the fledglings."[5]

Several exclusive fabrics were associated with the house during the 1880s. One, used for panels of dinner and reception dresses in 1881, was "a sort of embossed plush on a lapis blue satin ground, the plush forming rounds the size of the florin."[6] In the fall of 1882 a rich damask—violet with old-gold dahlias—was made up as a "Calypso" evening dress. Whether this is the same patterned fabric as found in two colorways in the Museum of the City of New York (38.220.12 and 31.3.4) is not known, but the colors—bright aqua combined with peach and white and crimson and white—are certainly appropriate to the period (fig. 1.79). As an English author put it, the Parisians had discovered the secret of uniting the most rebellious colors—plum and sky

1.78 (*Opposite*) Eastman Johnson (1824–1906) portrayed Mrs. Charles Mather Henderson in 1883 in her Worth gown patterned with tulips. Chicago Historical Society, Gift of Mrs. Robert Gay, 1954.249 (Dress: 1957. 525.)

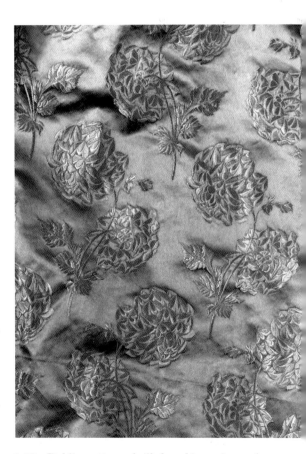

1.79 Dahlia-patterned silk found in various colorways in Worth garments. Museum of the City of New York, Gift of Francis H. Markoe, 31.3.4.

blue, yellow and bronze, pink and red, and blue and green—with the last two joined together in nature so successfully, but elsewhere not always.[7] Worth had a color preference in the early 1880s for combinations of brown and russet, dark green and brown, and in one instance in 1883, he melded brocaded satin of "pepita yellow" with shrimp pink ottoman silk, trimming it with bows of chaudron (antique red) velvet ribbon.[8] Worth to this day is credited with never pronouncing a color fashionable, but, rather, selecting the particular shade suitable to his client—or so the world was led to believe.

As for fabrics and trims in the eighties, there seems to have been a place for everything. Worth championed the return of velvets—plain, cut, stamped, and others—often combining them with other fabrics such as the newly modish Sicilienne, one of the family of ribbed silks known as faille, bengaline, grosgrain, and ottoman, "very soft and supple and no warmer than velvet or brocade, or Persian silk."[9]

The fabric riot that continued for much of the 1880s was fed on pattern, and in dressmaking such patterned goods were layered, textured, and mixed and matched. They encased ladies in the most upholstered look of all time: with the back bustle projection, many festive balls must have looked like a waltz of musical chairs. In the minority of Worth garments of the early 1880s are those of plain fabrics carrying holdover labels of the 1870s. Florals predominated, either with the house's perennial favorite, tulips, or in various floral displacements. The house's selection of botanicals even included realistic interpretations of the leaves and acorn seeds of the stately oak (The Brooklyn Museum, 61.16). Bold stripes were woven in monochrome, ombré, or vivid Roman-ribbon color and pattern, and Renaissance-revival motifs began to appear. Late eighteenth-century floral embroidery motifs were reinterpreted as borders.

Following the design excesses of the early years of the 1880s—an almost junglelike mingling of pattern on pattern and a bombardment of textures and trims, wherein baubles, beads, and bows fight for supremacy among the fringe—the restraint observed in many of the garments from the mid-1880s seems to match that of their labels. Plain fabrics, especially satins in black and whites, returned, along with a general accent on heavy, crisp, shiny fabrics. Dynamic circles and marquise-shaped motifs, in keeping with the impressive substance of the fabric, were introduced.

At least three textiles used by Worth can at present be directly related to specific weaving establishments. Tellingly, all three were exhibition-quality designs, as it is through exhibition records that the trail of production can be traced. (Samples of all three can be seen at the Musée Historique des Tissus, Lyon.) Perhaps one of the most remarkable textiles ever used by the house was woven in 1888–89 by A. Gourd & Cie of Lyon; the fabric (Musée Historique des Tissus, 24.89.2) was distributed in Paris by Morel, Poeckès, &

1.80 *"Chrysanthemums,"* woven by J. Bachelard & Cie for the Exposition Universelle of 1894. The fabric advertised in this sketch is a broché damask. The gown is by Worth.

Baumlin. Entitled "Tulipes Hollandaises," it was included in the section of Lyonnaise textiles at the Exposition Universelle of 1889, garnering a grand prix for Maison Gourd. Worth employed the fabric in an evening cape, a "Sortie de Bal" that belonged to one of the Hewitt sisters (pl. 8). With its thirty-one-inch spread between tulip-spray repeats, it displays Worth's adroitness in using uncommonly bold motifs. For the period, this wrap shows a noticeable restraint in its trim, which consists of only a few tassels nestled in a flounced yoke and collar of shirred black Chantilly lace. Otherwise the fabric is left to fall uninterruptedly from shoulder to hem in an all-enveloping cape. With the silhouetting black satin ground, the effect is a botanical celebration: fireworks of flowers in vibrant reds and golds and softer mossy greens. Harmonizing well in color and texture is a soft dusty rose silk-velvet lining.

The second fabric is a windblown vertical spread of chrysanthemums in all stages of bloom. This *grand damas broché* came from the looms of J. Bachelard & Cie, also of Lyon, and was exhibited by them at the 1894 Exposition Universelle held in Lyon. Unfortunately the exhibition sample, now at the Musée Historique des Tissus (25.823) does not offer a complete motif repeat, but it appears to be the textile of an evening-dress skirt sketched at the time (fig. 1.80).

1.81 Swallows in a seascape swoop across a damask silk woven by Les Petit-Fils de C. F. Bonnet & Cie of Lyon. The evening coat is by Worth.

1.82 (*Opposite*) An elegant ball gown of sky blue damask brocaded with a charming design of chrysanthemum petals is fashioned of the same fabric as Mrs. Perry's coordinated three-piece evening outfit (pls. 10, 11). As sketched by A. Sandoz, it was published on the cover of *Harper's Bazar*, April 15, 1893.

1.83 Textile panels of silk pile pattern on satin ground, from a Worth garment of about 1900. The Brooklyn Museum, Museum Purchase 1985.207.

The Worth connection with the Bonnet looms is indicated by the third textile, of swallows swooping over a seascape (Musée Historique des Tissus, 31.062). The fabric, a pink silk damask, warp-printed with gray-blue birds, measuring 62 centimeters selvedge to selvedge, with a 59-centimeter repeat, was also featured in the 1894 exhibition. The material was fashioned by Worth into a popular, and long fashionable, evening wrap with broad, plainly faced shawl collar and full, fluted sleeves that would accommodate dress sleeves of any shoulder-line fullness (fig. 1.81).

Whether Worth introduced a collection of models developed around fabrics with interrelated motifs is not known. However, from the period between 1889 and 1894 comes another chrysanthemum pattern—just fluttering petals—that is to be found in a three-piece evening ensemble (pls. 10, 11; fig. 1.82), and a swallow-patterned silk. The swallow silk is woven *en disposition* as a deep border, a breathtaking Provençal sunset, the satin ground ombré-shaded from hot reds at the top to cold purple blues at the bottom. Across this rainbowed sky, blue, blue-green, black, gray-white, and orange swallows dart and dive (Musée Historique des Tissus, 25.824).

1.84 Tassel fabric associated with the House of Worth found woven in two techniques and dimensions. Museum of the City of New York, unaccessioned.

Two instances of motifs with variants in different scales are known. One is a marquise or elliptical form woven in at least two scales, where measurements vary by 10 centimeters.[10] The larger-scale fabric is believed to have been first introduced in about 1887. Whether the fabrics of the two gowns were marketed simultaneously is not known, as The Brooklyn Museum's example (pl. 5) has not only an earlier cut but an earlier label. It also has the larger pattern of the two renditions, which was eminently suitable to the proportions of the matriarch who sailed forth in the production. The second instance concerns a "tassel" fabric. Two variants of the larger-scale yard goods remain, and on one, smaller tassels have been cut out from a smaller-scale fabric and appliquéd to the sample (fig. 1.84).[11] These pieces were available in two qualities—one highlighted with silver threads, the second woven only in bright gold silk.

Included in the Storch and Martin 1889 Exposition Universelle commemorative album highlighting the silk-weaving industry of Lyon are two textiles executed for court wear having no known association with Worth but whose splendor and style are suggestive of the house. The first is a lampas with a satin ground, in the Louis XVI manner, with an elongated cluster of three plumes among a variety of floral sprays. It was the product of MM. J. M. Piotet & Roque. The second was a court-trained mantle woven by Maison Bernard & Ferrand on a jacquard loom—a textile reminiscent of ogivally configured medieval brocaded velvets. Framing the alternating rows of elliptal leaf forms are bands of grosgrain patterned with the effect of embroidered flowers. The palms or broad, flat leaves with serrated edges had a satin ground, in which the multiblossomed, stylized floral sprays were worked in either gold or silver lamé. A number of other 1889 Bernard & Ferrand silks—grand-scale and realistic renditions of gladiola, phlox, roses, lilies—are very much in keeping with house tastes.[12]

It would seem justifiable to assume that the looms of other skillful Lyonnaise weavers fabricated textiles that found their way into Worth garments, either directly or through middlemen merchants such as Morel, Poeckès & Baumlin or Bradford & Perrier, both of Paris. Bradford & Perrier, active 1875 through at least 1901, were suppliers of the highest-quality silks and other textiles to the leading dressmaking houses of the day, including Worth. Mr. Bradford would make biannual buying trips to Lyon, where he would acquire exclusive designs from a number of manufacturers. Other weavers for Worth may have included Bresson, Agrees & Cie; Audibert & Cie; Pancet, Père et Fils; Bardon & Fitton & Mayon; but a most likely candidate is Devaux et Bachelard, who wove a nighttime skyscape with white-to-gray cumulus clouds interspersed with silver-thread stars set against a gray-blue satin ground.[13] Skyscapes fascinated the house.

Of the extant garments reviewed, a remarkably large number were executed in the same fabric, albeit usually in different colorways, or, in one instance, in mirror-image technique. A 1902–3 evening dress belonging to Caroline Schermerhorn Astor Wilson was fashioned from a cream silk satin with black velvet rose-leaf clusters in which a smattering of black velvet rose blossoms fall at the hemline. The same motif of leaves and roses is incorporated in two evening coats, one remodeled (The Metropolitan Museum of Art, 49.3.7, 61.43) and one known only from a photograph (Victoria and Albert Museum, Worth Archives, model no. 18779). The fabric of the coats also has the roses and leaves in satin, now surrounded by velvet grounds, one pale gray-green and the other only identified as green. Also known are two memorable Art Nouveau designs. One, a stylized lily, is still found in dress form, in black on white (Philadelphia Museum of Art, 1977.182.1), and in skirt panels, in self-colored *eau de nile* (The Brooklyn Museum, 85.207) and in the model books (Victoria and Albert Museum, Worth Archives, model no. 4281). Again in velvet, on a satin ground, is a vibrant elongated Renaissance strapwork pattern, found in black on white (The Metropolitan Museum of Art, 1976.258.1), self-colored sea mist green (The Metropolitan Museum of Art, 57.17.8), and rose on white (Chicago Historical Society, 1959.190).

Of all the satin-ground damasks associated with Worth, perhaps the one demanding most scrutiny is now sadly only a series of skirt panels. It is silk damask woven *en disposition* in black on black. Configured with the triangular form of the skirt panel godets of the 1890s is a woven pyramid floral spray. The flowers are common enough—morning glories, poppies, moss roses—and are joined by a favorite house subject, the butterfly, but a slithering salamander comes as a surprise (Museum of the City of New York, unaccessioned).

Grains—wheat and maize—held fascination for the house designers, perhaps because these plants in their mature, tasseled state resemble another of the house's longstanding trademarks—feathers. The grains are presented in a greater variety of ways than the feathers, which tend to be woven or printed rather than brilliantly embroidered. In a skirt panel at the Museum of the City of New York, maize ears, leaves, and silk are executed in gilt metallic thread set off on an icy blue silk-satin ground.[14] The fabric probably dates to the early 1890s. Several evening dresses survive with wheat stalks embroidered in brilliants and other glittery glass. One dating to about 1898 from The Brooklyn Museum has the stones and beads applied in vertical arrangements on vivid orchid silk satin (pl. 18). Under gas- or candlelight the expanse of stalks must have resembled amber waves of grain as carried forth on Mrs. Arthur F. Schermerhorn. Mrs. William Astor, also at the turn of the century, possessed a grain-motif gown with a center-front sheaf that hardly leaves the grounding of the hemline (The Metropolitan Museum of Art, 49.3.10).

1.85 Although the gown belonging to Mrs. Perry (pl. 14) dates from 1894, the fabric selection had been available as early as 1892, as seen in the A. Sandoz sketch of Worth evening toilettes for the cover of *Harper's Bazar*, Sept. 24, 1892.

Attired, Mrs. Astor would have appeared as if walking through a field of crystallized grains. A less ambitious representation of the grains has arching, interlocking heads and stems. What seems like a small, confined pattern turns out to be like an almost endless prairie: the pattern repeat is over 280 centimeters in length (The Metropolitan Museum of Art, 56.32.10; Chicago

Historical Society, 1960.590). Evidence would suggest that Jean-Philippe Worth promoted ever-bolder and large-scale fabric motifs.

Feathers float through the years of the House of Worth (pl. 14, fig. 1.85). The majority of plumes are either curled ostrich or peacock and have been interpreted in a variety of ways. Two examples of the former may be seen in The Metropolitan Museum of Art and the Cooper-Hewitt Museum.[15] In the former, two tightly clustered, cloudlike stripes of deep cream feathers run up against a burnt orange silk moiré ground. The dual feather stripe is additionally to be found in "Plumes," a monochromatically printed velvet on a satin ground shown by Maison Brunet-Lecomte & Moïse at the 1889 Exposition Universelle. It is not now known if this freer interpretation of feathers was used by Worth, but it is certainly in Worth's taste. The Cooper-Hewitt material, in ever-changing shades of silver gray on silver gray, may well be the greatest amount of uncut yard goods associated with Worth; the Hewitt sisters bought the silk, now measuring 35 feet 10 inches in length, on one of their excursions to Paris. From about the same time comes a scale motif in shades of gray, also in the Cooper-Hewitt collection (fig. 1.86). The association with Worth can be made through fashion engravings published in 1888–89 (figs. 1.87, 1.88).

Feathers adorn several other fabrics associated by tradition with Worth and now housed in the Musée Historique des Tissus, Lyon. One is a skirt-front pyramid of cascading feathers worked in green cut velvet on a brassy gold ground (31.092); another is but half a mirror image of a similarly configured motif of three graduated clusters of black feathers caught in bows set against a tile red ground over which smaller feathers flutter (accession number unknown). These pieces were probably included in the 1894 Exposition, while exhibited in 1889 was a printed velvet by Ogier, Duplain & Cie of graduated peacock-plume eyes (accession number unknown).

An understanding of the play of colors and textures is one of the enduring achievements of the house, successfully passed from one generation to another. Worth used subtle, undulating hues rather than pure red, white, or blue. The selection of colors was one of the senior Worth's greatest talents; he would sweep aside fabric after fabric until the desired harmony was achieved. A correspondent wrote in 1873: "I have recently seen samples of pieces selected by Worth for winter toilettes. Besides silk velvets and velveteens, plain, but of the most singular shades, there were figured, printed and stamped velvets, and still other kinds. Some of these samples had a ground for black faille with damask designs (large running figures) of black raised velvet. Others were of olive bronze velvet, with very fine close stripes, alternating velvet and lusterless silk. Still others were of stamped velvet with a dark blue mottled ground, covered with a damask pattern formed of pale pink flowers and olive green foliage."[16]

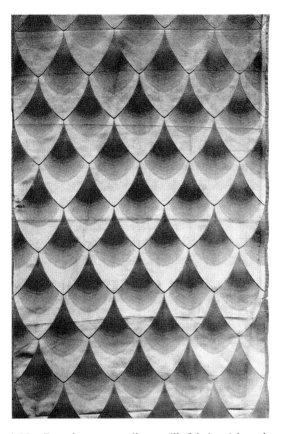

1.86 Complex-weave silvery silk fabric with scallop or scale motif associated with Worth garments from the late 1880s. Cooper-Hewitt Museum, Gift of Mrs. Harry T. Peters, 1956.82.2.

81

It seems to be a late twentieth-century misconception that in Victorian times black was reserved exclusively for the condition of mourning (fig. 1.89). A flounced lace frock was described in 1884 as one of Worth's costliest black dresses, and the lace trim was only imitation (meaning machine-made) Chantilly lace. Worth also created mourning attire, available in London at the specialty shop of Messrs. Jay. They carried "the newest French costumes imported" for occasions such as the 1884 state mourning for Queen Victoria's youngest son, Leopold, duke of Albany. In 1882 one of the "novelties" on hand was a mourning "Dinner Toilette, one of Worth's happiest conceptions,

1.87, 1.88 (*Opposite and right*) Renderings of a Worth polonaise swagged with jet executed in faille broché with scallops. These autumnal outfits were published in *L'Illustration* (figure seated center) and *L'Art et la mode* in 1889.

JONNARD

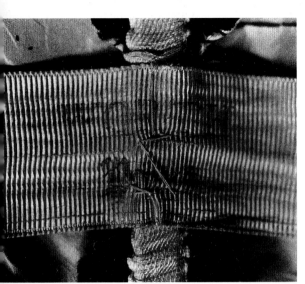

Fake Worth label, stamped gold on white
c. 1870s

1.89 Charles F. and/or Jean-Philippe Worth. *Evening Dress*, c. 1888. Black silk satin; jet bead trim, machine-made lace. Probably worn by Miss Sarah Hewitt. The Brooklyn Museum, Gift of the Princess Viggo in accordance with the wishes of the Misses Hewitt, 31.64.

in so much that the train remains important until its termination, without that draggled much-in-the-way appendage a train often assumes. In this instance the train looks stately whether you have a front or back view, for it is in fact double, which is a step towards perfection.''[17]

Many elaborate, specially commissioned embroideries were executed in the workshops of Albert Lesage. The most complicated and decorative were applied after the garment had been stitched together but before the final seam, giving three-dimensionality, was done. This construction technique allowed for an unbroken sweep of embroidery, as can be seen on a Worth gown in quintessentially French Rococo taste of pale aqua silk satin studded with crystal and diamanté beads, silver thread, and cording (The Metropolitan Museum of Art, 1975.251.4) and a remarkable wintertime late-afternoon dress of faux Venetian gros point lace fabricated from appliquéd wool broadcloth and silk twist cording laid on a crushed velvet ground (pl. 21). This technique had been applied to a carriage and indoor black dress in 1881 when Worth had employed hand embroidery in chenille pink moss roses and pale green foliage on a black satin dress with a pink satin *balayeuse* and draped with jetted net and lace.[18]

Later the House was to engage the services of René Begué, called Rébé, for embroidery. After working under the embroiderer Vitet, he began his business in 1911 and was employed by the likes of Dior, Fath, Balençiaga, Schiaparelli, Doeuillet, Poiret, and Doucet until closing in 1966. To Rébé, Jean-Philippe Worth of all his clients was ''l'artiste.''

Laces were but another arena in which Worth encouraged innovative manufacturers. With the technology to produce net mechanically well established in the late eighteenth century, it was only a matter of time before machine-made laces were on the market in the 1840s. Some were skeptical: ''Lace is always pretty when it is real; but as everyone cannot afford real lace, we shall see a quantity of common lace, which will give more of a common look to the dress than elegance.''[19] While Worth and his clients may have preferred trimmings of real (handmade) lace, over ninety percent of the extant garments reviewed for this project are embellished with mechanically made lace, either completely or, infrequently, in part.[20] The full gamut of lacemaking techniques and decorative styles is represented. Sometimes a revival derivative garment is even finished with appropriately modeled laces, as is common on seventeenth-century-styled tea gowns of the late 1890s and early 1900s. An array of such tea gowns in black silk was left by sisters Alice and Emma P. Foster to the Wadsworth Atheneum, Hartford (42.490–.504).

The reign of the House of Worth roughly coincides with the extreme popularity of lace in the nineteenth and twentieth centuries; lace's fall from favor came almost simultaneously with the stock-market crash of 1929. For generations women, in particular, had been advised that real lace was one of the best investments that could be made. In a few instances, particularly on Worth wedding dresses, one can discern stitching evidence of where real or heirloom lace was once applied. A now rather stark and severe off-white outfit from the 1870s in the Philadelphia Museum of Art (unaccessioned) was probably a wedding dress, whose silhouette was once softened with an edging and flounces of genuine needle or bobbin lace.

Most authors, including the head of the house, Jean-Philippe Worth, would have posterity believe that nearly every commission left the salons saturated with real lace. Extant garments (constituting only a fraction of those made) and the house model photograph albums, however, indicate only an occasional application of client-supplied laces, presumably heirloom real laces. In those cases the expenditure for *dentelle*, or lace, is much reduced or eliminated on an order. Perhaps both Maison Worth and the client hoped that the house-supplied lace was so cunningly made as to deceive all but the most experienced eye. This raises the question of why the Hewitt sisters prepared sample cards[21] with snippets of very typical machine-made lingerie laces removed from the understructures (dust ruffles and train flounces) of their Worth gowns, when many far more interesting examples existed. Counterbalancing the use of machine-made lace is the house's sensivity to the valued appreciation of a genuine piece of Brussels bobbin lace: around 1900, when the house made up a hip-length cape from lace that probably originally served as an altar cloth or frontal, not a thread was snipped. If the garment, now in the Fashion Institute of Technology collection, New York (69.190.9), were unpicked today, the lace could be returned to its original function.[22] The laces Worth employed show no hint of the design vocabulary of Art Nouveau, present in other areas of the house's textile design; the majority are either derivatives or adaptations of historical prototypes, but some are fabricated in currently fashionable techniques.

Glittering stones frequently blinded witnesses on the true value of applied decoration, and such false illusion has led to many misconceptions about Worth creations. Many believe that real jewels adorned the garments. Indeed it was written in 1889 that well-known dressmakers—Worth, Felix, Dusuzeau, Raudnitz—as well as lesser-known ones—Guillot, Barblet, Daltrope, Pingat, Sarah Meyer, and Pasquier—asked to know what kinds of jewels were to be worn with dresses "issued" by them, thus avoiding clashing combinations in the toilette.[23] But this reference obviously pertains to accessories of real jewels. In at least two instances reference is made to Worth's incorporation of gemstones in garments. Jean-Philippe claims Mme Musard, whose fortune came from oil discovered on land given to her by the king of the Netherlands, made available to the house, on a weekly basis, a selection of the jewels with which she wished to decorate her bodices for evening and opera engagements. And earlier, for the inclusion in the 1889

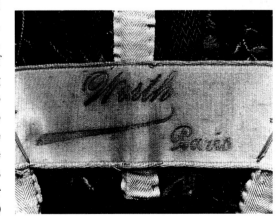

Fake Worth label, stamped gold on white c. 1880s

Paris Exposition, the Houses of Worth and Cartier collaborated on a jeweled evening outfit that Leopold, king of Belgium, later was to acquire and subsequently pass on.

Such cases were not the rule, however. Perhaps the myth of authentically bejeweled gowns was the result of attributions such as the following: "Mrs. Parkinson Sharp wore a beautiful Worth toilette of royal purple velvet, her cloak lined with sables, and ornaments of rubies and pearls."[24] Here the commentator probably speaks figuratively, to convey extended opulence, about an appliquéd motif actually composed of faceted, red-colored glass beads and spherical, opaquely coated hollow glass beads.

It is not known which member of the Worth family advocated using fabrication requirements as decorative finishes and edgings, and construction hardware as decorative features, though both would suggest the impulse of the junior Worth, who seems to have become a driving design force in the house in the late 1880s. External seams and edging on many of the most sumptuous evening gowns composed of intricate yet monumental silk patterning are found to be nothing more than the humble fabric selvedge. As a house design device, this technique continued for several decades. Hooks and eyes—washed in gold, enlarged, and decorated—were favored as trimmings, serving as alternatives for silk or wool-braided brandenburgs (see fig. 1.63).[25]

Goods and novelties procured from outside the house—some ready-made, some just in bulk—included passementerie, fringes, floral decorations, embroideries, beads and baubles, and feathers and furs. All elements necessary to production were centrally gathered and then some fabricating was farmed out, with the cutting and fittings taking place within the rue de la Paix establishment.

✥⫸∘⫷✥ ✥⫸∘⫷✥ ✥⫸∘⫷✥ ✥⫸∘⫷✥

CLIENTS

The allure of a Worth garment for thousands of clients was perhaps summed up by Lillie Moulton, who emphasized not only the external aspects of one gown but also the name literally attached to it: "I thought it was best to make a good impression at the start [for her first invitation to the French court in 1866] so I put on my prettiest gown. . . . If one could see the waist band, one would read Worth in big letters."[1] Another American customer, Marion

"Clover" Adams (1843–85) rather bravely, and perhaps overenthusiastically, wrote, "What doesn't show is as good as what does, so that when the right side is quite worn out I shall simply wear the wrong side out."[2] Mrs. Adams had begun her communication by rhapsodizing, "My Worth gown has come home and not only fills my soul but seals it hermetically. Still it has enough air about it to prevent suffocation."[3]

Rich, regal (whether royal or theatrical), and raffish—such was the composition of the house's clientele. Although Charles Frederick Worth was never taken into the social milieu of his titled customers in a manner that is almost an expected prerogative of today's monarchs of fashion, clients considered his word absolute within the confines of the fashion fortress at 7 rue de la Paix. Few dared protest, as did Mrs. Oliphant in her 1878 book, *The Art of Dress*: "We were not born under M. Worth's sway. He is not our natural monarch, but yet we obey him like slaves. . . . The first thing we have to consider is whether there is any reasonable and likely way of getting free."[4] Her challenge fell on deaf American ears. Nor did they heed Mrs. John Sherwood, who in *Manners and Social Usages* railed against the orange, blue, pink and lilac lace-flounced dresses of Worth and Pingat and cast her contempt on women who would wear such showpieces in public without a shrouding mantle.[5]

Indeed, the woman who was drawn to Worth not only wore showpieces but, in accordance with the feminine ideal of her time, was something of a showpiece herself. The ideal woman in the 1880s, when Rubensesque physical attributes carried the cultural connotation of health and prosperity, would tip the scales between 140 and 160 pounds, while standing only five foot three inches tall. As numerous advertisements for wire-form bust improvers and additions of cotton-wool pads to bodices testify, less than liberally endowed late nineteenth-century ladies were not above enhancing nature (fig. 1.90). Indeed, the corset encouraged the accentuation of the breasts by pushing them up and out and at the same time providing support for them and the back. The goal of encasement in corsetry was the hourglass silhouette with diminutive waist and flaring hips counterbalancing the bustline. Where and when necessary, bustles and tonures could also be worn for plumping out the back bottom region. At the same time, popularly held notions that eighteen-inch waist circumferences were the norm in the mid- and late nineteenth century are without confirmation through extant garments. Even more interesting, in most of extant pairs of bodices for a single skirt (Worth's included), the less formal or long-sleeved one will measure smaller at both the bust and waistline than the décolleté evening one.[6] The allowance of extra room might be attributable to the enjoyment of either meals or exposed bosom, depending on point of view. Even though the displacement of the waistline might vary—sometimes high, sometimes low, sometimes natural—

ÊTRE ET PARAITRE, par Hadol.

1.90 Cutaway revealing the structuring of a woman supporting the dictates of fashion. Sketch by Hadol, 1869.

Fake Worth label, stamped gold on white with
"2 Rue de la Paix" address
c. 1905

skirt waistbands usually measure greater in circumference than bodice waistlines since skirts were designed to sit just below the "waist" so as not to add bulk to this focal area. During the 1890s, from a point of view of health, there was a general reappraisal of "beauty," especially as it was perceived in stout women. Because most of Worth's customers were lifelong patrons, however, surviving garments tend to have matronly proportions. Catering to middle-age spread was important to Maison Worth since, as Lucy Hooper wrote in 1892, "Half of the beauties that first brought his toilettes into vogue have become faded old ladies, and the rest are no longer living."[7]

Aside from mighty and minor crowned heads, the house's most conspicuous clients were probably newly moneyed Americans, including fictional ladies of literature. As early as 1865, the popular American publication *Peterson's Magazine* carried a mercifully short story, "Miss Woggles' Wardrobe," in which the heroine—an heiress, of course—vainly attempts to deflect the wandering eye of her suitor by wearing "her most exquisite Parisian dresses, dresses that the great Worth himself had made."[8] In Mrs. Sherwood's *A Transplanted Rose* (1882), the small-town, western heroine first faces New York society in a "blazing brocade" made by a hometown seamstress but eventually wins not only the hand of an English lord but also a Worth trousseau as well. Louisana, from the novel of that name by Frances Hodgson Burnett (1880), is a country bumpkin, unaware of the seductive effects of a Worth, much less his name, as she is cajoled into trying on a cream silk evening dress. Miraculously it fits: "There was not a shadow of a wrinkle from shoulder to hem: the lovely young figure was revealed in all its beauty of outline. There were no sleeves at all, there was not very much bodice, but there was a great deal of effect."[9] Imitating the dissatisfaction of real clients, fictional ones also felt betrayed. A Mrs. Spring spoke up: "I shall never trust Worth again. He has lost all conscience. He seems to think that anything is good enough for America."[10] Fictional characters and their Worths promenade through all levels of literary endeavor, appearing in the novels of Edith Wharton, herself an expatriate client. In *The Age of Innocence*, Mrs. Baxter Pennilow "did everything handsomely [and] used to import twelve a year.... It was a standing order, and as she was ill for two years before she died they found forty eight Worth dresses that had never been taken out of tissue paper . . ."[11] So as not to appear ostentatious, she would let new garments mellow their shocking newness for a year.

Perhaps the rapport achieved with Americans can be directly related to the fact that the elder Worth never totally mastered the French tongue and that he too was a self-made man with expensive tastes. In conversation with F. Adolphus in the early 1870s, he explained why he appreciated Americans: "They have faith, figures and francs,—faith to believe in me, figures that I can put into shape, francs to pay my bills."[12] Mrs. M. E. W. Sherwood reiterates the point in *The American Code of Manners* (1884): "Worth says, that American women are the best customers he has—far better than queens. *They* ask the price; American women never do. They simply say, 'Give me the best, the most beautiful, the most fashionable gown!'"[13]

Socially ambitious, American women had been early and consistent clients of the House of Worth, perhaps even assisting during the short setback at the time of the Siege of Paris. Lillie Moulton[14] even wrote of an aborted visit on March 20, 1871:

> I happened to go at one o'clock to Worth's. . . . [Finding the street barred] I walked quickly . . . and hardly had I reached his salon than we heard distant confused sounds [which] made us all rush to the windows. [The crowd] seeing people on Worth's balcony beckoned them to join . . . but Mr. Worth wisely withdrew inside and shaking his Anglo-Saxon head, said, 'Not I.' *HE*, indeed. . . . One can't imagine the horror we felt when we heard the roar of a cannon. . . . The street was filled with dead and wounded. I felt terribly agitated; my one thought was to reach my carriage [left on the rue St. Arnaud]. The rue de la Paix was, of course, impossible, Worth had a courtyard, but no outlet into the rue St. Arnaud. He suggested that I go through his 'ateliers,' which he had at the top of the house, and reach the adjoining apartment, from which I might descend to the rue St. Arnaud. . . . He told one of his women to lead the way, and I followed. We toiled up many flights of wearisome steps until we arrived at the above mentioned ateliers . . . I . . . descended the five flights of waxed steps, holding onto the wobbly iron railing."[15]

The Americans were not always the most lavish spenders at Maison Worth, but they were valued patrons nonetheless. Estimating in 1871 that the average client spent between £400 and £4,000 per annum on purchases from his house, Worth indicated that top honors for expenditure went to the Russians, not so much the current empress as the grand duchesses—especially Grand Duchess Marie. He continued:

Fake Worth label. Woven 1910

> It doesn't run in nations, exactly. Often it's a Russian . . . or it's an American. Sometimes it's a Peruvian or a Chilean; sometimes, even it's a French woman, though the French are usually rather careful; economy is in the blood, you know. Here and there a Spaniard or a Southern Italian may turn prodigal, or people of some of the out-lying races. But rarely does an Englishwoman get really wasteful, and I have not known a single case of a German reaching any such amount as I am talking of. Some of the Americans are great spenders; all of them (all of them that I see, I mean) love dress, even if they are not extravagant over it.[16]

Mrs. Sherwood said it was no wonder that an American lady sent to France for her clothes, for the ordering is simplified, the customer is assured of good material, a good fit, and stylish clothes at half their cost in New York.[17]

Isabella Gardner and Clover Adams echoed their agreement from Boston. American dressmakers were accused of being both drunks and not proficient at fitting clothes. At Worth, American clients pressed for and were granted individual consideration. Jean-Philippe Worth recalled that it became quite the thing, especially with American customers, never to look at models:[18] the clients preferred the attention of the master, who would drape fabrics as he described an imagined design in a tongue they readily comprehended.

Worth found that American women "more frequently than in the women of any other nation had slimness without leanness. Leanness, sometimes called scrawniness, he abhorred."[19] Seconding his approval, late nineteenth-century American journalists were repetitive in their remarks that the fair daughters of Uncle Sam were the only foreigners who had the gift of being able to wear a Parisian toilette—particularly the capricious, arrogant New York society women (who found Worth client Edith Wharton too serious to be fashionable, while Boston saw her as too fashionable to be serious). According to the journalists, the American woman saw what Paris had, and adapted what she pleased, fixing what "her sex all over the land shall wear or try to wear."[20] It should be noted, however, that the fashion correspondents usually qualified this praise by explaining that "contrary to the general impression . . . it is not the great couturiers, tailors and modists, such as Felix, Laferrière, Worth, Virot etc. who decree the fashions, but the great ladies of the old world. By reason of their birth and breeding they possess an innate taste as well as a sense of refined and harmonious elegance in which the former are lamentably deficient, and hence the new creations . . . never really become fashionable . . . until after they have under gone those modifications by the great ladies, which are needed to deprive them of their pristine vulgarity and consequent lack of true chic and elegance."[21]

Nevertheless, Americans were a strong presence at the Worth salons. In 1888 a visitor to the house recorded his impressions:

> It is October, and Paris is full of foreigners. The King of Dress holds a levée daily from two until five P.M., no. 7 rue de la Paix, first story above the "entresol." He is the only absolute monarch left in Europe, and his court is the most cosmopolitan. . . .
>
> Mr. Worth himself is the center of constantly changing groups of men and women, American, English, French, Russian, Spanish & unclassified. They are not all speaking or listening to him—only those who understand English or can guess at his French can do that; the others are waited upon by underlings, who address them in their native language. But the majority cluster round Mr. Worth. He is dressed in a blue flannel sack-coat, buttoned across his burly person, brown trousers, a turned down collar and crimson scarf, all shabby. The immediate object of his attention is a single lady of great wealth, from New York; grey haired,

quiet in dress and demeanor, but with something about her which marks her as being somebody, as distinguished from anybody.[22]

On another occasion, an observer wrote, "There was not one word of French to be heard among the ladies who were grouped in the various rooms holding conclave together about the grand affair on hand; *they were all American.*"

One such American was Isabella Stewart Gardner (fig. 1.91), who eventually deserted the house for the newly established House of Paquin just months after the death of the senior Worth in 1895, but not before the spotlight had fallen on her in numerous Worth creations: an early 1895 black costume, magnificent, but very simple, for a papal interview; an 1874 mourning dress, black again, but drawing comment on line; an 1881–82 white uncut-velvet ball gown worn when "chandeliering" (waltzing in the center of the ballroom); an 1868 street costume having bands of sealskins with matching sealskin jacket, muff, and hat; and, also from 1868, a short dress, six inches off the ground. To her eye, Worth gowns were as beautifully finished inside as out, perhaps setting up a legendary retort attributed to Tom Appleton: "Pray, who undressed you?" he is said to have asked. "Worth," said Mrs. Jack. "Didn't he do it well!"[23]

Like many American clients, Isabella Gardner eagerly shared her enthusiasm for Worth with friends who may have been as influenced by names as by the gowns. On September 21, 1879, Clover Adams wrote her father: "Henry and I were presented in great form to the Great Mr. Worth by Mrs. Gardner. Mr. Worth ordered one of his young women to parade in a gown designed for the Grand Duchess of Wurtemburg." Mrs. Adams "so far yielded to Henry's wishes as to order a duplicate gown" in dark green merino trimmed with dark blue. The grand duchess's had been blue merino with black satin. Observing another client in the salon that day, the Adamses judged him "a compatriot, [perhaps] a prosperous grocer from Iowa with a fat wife for whom he wanted a smart dress. To see him in his spruce broadcloth frock coat and awe-struck expression, hefting the silks to be sure he was getting his money's worth, and finally examining for himself shelf after shelf of pieces was an inspiring spectacle."[24] Late in 1879 Mrs. Adams was to write: "Yesterday I went to consult Mr. Worth about a gown to go with my Louis XIV lace, which he admired extremely, as I knew he would. . . . This is what he wants me to have: the main dress gold color, the velvet only to lay the lace on and at the bottom in front. I have become bored with the idea of getting any new gowns, but Henry says, 'People who study Greek must take pains with their dress.' If I were a bonanzaine I would sail in and make a business of it, but an occasional venture is too much trouble."[25] What Clover Adams could not buy directly she tried to cajole her father into transporting: "Pass a week in Paris, and I'll write ahead to Worth for some gowns, and you

1.91 Isabella Stewart Gardner, a Worth client for over thirty years, as photographed c. 1888 by J. Thomson, London.

1.92 Miss Eleanor Gurnee Hewitt (Miss Nelly), one of three daughters of Abram Hewitt and Sarah Amelia Cooper. Slightly smaller than her sister, Miss Sally, she dressed a bit mannishly and especially admired the needle arts.

1.93 (*Right*) Princess Viggo (née Eleanor M. Green), daughter of Amelia (Amy) and niece of Sarah and Eleanor Hewitt, dressed in a Worth probably worn by Miss Nelly in about 1882. (Dress, The Brooklyn Museum, Gift of the Princess Viggo, 31.31.)

1.94 Miss Sarah Hewitt (Miss Sally) was enormous and amusing, and with her collecting instincts for textiles, she made an ideal armature for the display of bold Worth creations.

bring them back to me."[26] The Boston belles, Gardner and Adams, concurred that the house's prices were as reasonable as dressmakers' prices in Boston.

When the Hewitt sisters of New York were being fitted, the house had a stepladder available, so that Miss Eleanor (Nelly) (fig. 1.92) and Miss Sarah (Sally) (fig. 1.94) could test out the garments they would be wearing as they clambered about in the library of their museum. Early in their lives, they—along with their mother, Mrs. Abram Stevens Hewitt (née Sarah Amelia Cooper) and sister Amelia (Amy)—had been taken with the "French taste," which stimulated regular visits to Europe. Numerous garments from their wardrobes, ranging in date from the early 1880s into the early twentieth century, were given to New York City museums in the early 1930s (fig. 1.93). Unfortunately many are marred with alterations. Most pieces bear a Worth label, although the Hewitts were occasionally lured to the salons of other houses. The House of Worth particularly suited their dressing demands since for many years it specialized in garments adapted from eighteenth-century women's riding outfits, in turn derived from the cut of a man's body coat. Worth even went so far as to make women's jackets from the elaborately decorated men's dress coats of a century earlier. Such pieces were literally made to order for Miss Nelly, who dressed a bit mannishly and has been described as smaller, more feminine, and more athletic than Sally; interested in everything that went on; and a wizard with her needle. Several of her late nineteenth-century Worth suits survive with Rococo- and Neoclassical-inspired embroidery decoration carried out in silks and spangles (pl. 17); the latter, in one instance, were silver-dusted cardboard discs (see fig. 1.64).

Sarah Hewitt has been characterized as having the quicker intelligence, sharper eye, and more amusing manner of the two sisters. She has also been described as "enormous," but the sisters' garments are of average proportions for Worth clients of their age and time. Miss Sally favored the very large-scale fabric motifs for which Worth was known, and the house contributed textile samples to the Hewitts' museum collection (now in the Cooper-Hewitt Museum).

The alterations many of the Hewitts' garments underwent may explain the remarks of their friends. The art dealer Germain Seligman observed that as they grew older, "they retained the patterns of their youth, and the sumptuous materials of their gowns were still fashioned in the old modes as were their hats!"[27] And Allyn Cox noted them "in green and purple patterns. They were quite a sight!"[28]

It is not always possible to distinguish which of the four Hewitt ladies wore a given extant garment, but cuts and materials reveal preferences for floral motifs, especially roses; adaptations of historic textiles; and eighteenth-century-style garments rather than house workhorses of seventeenth-century inspiration.[29]

The Hewitts' friends of Mrs. J. (Frances) Pierpont Morgan (fig. 1.95) and her three daughters also shopped at Worth. The family tradition had begun a generation earlier, when Junius Spencer Morgan and his wife Juliet had both befriended Worth and become his clients. J. P. Morgan himself usually accompanied the distaff members of the family on shopping expeditions, encouraging purchases. Frances was shy, quiet, and timid, with no desire for display except as it pleased her husband. Jean-Philippe Worth felt she never would have come to the house of her own volition, though her husband regarded it as the sole couturier establishment.[30] It was Morgan, rather than his wife, who selected the Worth fabrics and fashions that were made into their daughter Louisa's 1900 trousseau. In 1902 daughters Anne and Juliet bought two nearly identical gowns of pale yellowish satin covered with satin and French-knot embroidery (The Metropolitan Museum of Art, New York, 52.60.6; Union Française des Arts du Costume, Paris, 78.2.10).

At the very head of New York society was the famed Mrs. Astor, Caroline Webster Schermerhorn Astor (Mrs. William Backhouse Astor, Jr.) and her daughter Caroline (Carrie) Schermerhorn Astor. They have left telling raiment: the mother's costly, almost larger than life, and formidable; and the

1.95 Jean-Philippe Worth. *Evening Gown*, 1902. Silk tulle, embroidered dragonflies in blue-black beadwork. Worn by Mrs. J. P. Morgan. Museum of the City of New York, Gift of Mrs. J. J. Crain, 44.7.

1.96 The pinnacle of the pyramid of women's clubs was attained by Mrs. Potter Palmer, who achieved international fame in 1893 as chairman of the Women's Pavilion at the World's Columbian Exposition. Her Worth wardrobe provided attire appropriate for a multitude of functions. The leaf-patterned silk-velvet gown shown here dates to c. 1900 and can be matched to a garment in the Worth model photograph archives, no. 29.

daughter's less commanding in scale and presence. One need only look at Carolus-Duran's portrait of Mrs. Astor (see fig. 1.62) wearing the very image of a seventeenth-century gown, to see that she was a model Worth client. Through marriage, Carrie was related to Consuelo Vanderbilt, whose wedding dress is one of the seemingly few gowns for a marriage between money and title that Worth had no hand in fabricating: rather, it was an American copy of a gown from one of Worth's chief competitors, Doucet.

American social arbiter of the day Ward McAllister recommended the house for packaging daughters who were to be launched into Society, whether in New York or London. Max Beerbohm had seen "pretty creatures clad in Worth's most elegant confections" invade London Society in early 1880.[31] Wherever money was being made, Worths were to be found. Women of Cleveland and Cincinnati were early enthusiasts, and perhaps one of the earliest and youngest was Kate Chase (later Mrs. William Sprague), wife of the governor of Ohio, who in the 1870s was deemed to be the most fashionable woman in the United States. *Demorest's Magazine* describes her as outshining the bride at her sister's wedding in 1871, to which the red-headed Mrs. Chase wore a costume of nile-green faille, with a train of rose-pink faille trimmed with green ruche. Other Cincinnati names associated with Worth from the first twenty years of business are Mrs. Joseph C. Thoms, Mrs. Murat Halstead, and Mrs. Robert Fulton Leaman.

Later came the Chicago clients. Taken as a group, the garments of Bertha Honoré Palmer (Mrs. Potter Palmer) (fig. 1.96), chairman of the Woman's Pavilion of the World's Columbian Exposition of 1893, are outstandingly harmonious, elegant, and reflective of the finest qualities of Worth. She favored the house's rich expressions of decoration and fabric. Her more conservative fellow Chicagoans Nancy (Nettie) McCormick (figs. 1.97, 1.98) and Abbie Louise Spencer Eddy (see fig. 3.6) also included Worths in their wardrobes. And on the West Coast, another energetic patron was to be found in Jane (Mrs. Leland) Stanford (see fig. 3.7).

As Worth's costumes had been championed at the French court, it has been assumed that Empress Eugénie was his first royal endorser. This honor, according to Lucy Hooper, belongs instead to Donna Maria da Gloria, queen regnant of Portugal.[32] Nevertheless, the names of Eugénie and Worth are permanently entwined. From a minor titled family (her parents were the count and countess of Teba, later styled Montijo de Guzman), she became, with her marriage to Napoleon III, heiress presumptive to Josephine and the scintillating aura of France under the First Empire. Louis Napoleon's father was, after all, Napoleon's brother, Louis, king of the Netherlands, who had been married to Hortense, Josephine's spirited daughter by her first marriage. Napoleon III actually encouraged his wife's patronage of Worth and other dressmakers of the day; he would reproach her for her simple tastes, which are hardly reflected in the tulle-clouded confections in which she appeared at state functions. Many of those who knew Eugénie emphasize, however, that she was not absorbed by the subject of clothes.

A true picture of the scope of the Empress's wardrobe is hard to come by, as much is only revealed through the envious eyes of contemporaries. It has been reported that on semiofficial occasions several new outfits were required daily—for both the Empress and her guests. Couturiers and *modistes*, it is recollected, were in constant attendance, yet when Eugénie was forced into exile, only about "three score completely new dresses ready to be put on" were found and forwarded to her at Chiselhurst, the royal family's place of exile in England.[33]

A watercolor design (fig. 1.99) that belonged to a series of Worth watercolor sketches before that series entered the Victoria and Albert Museum, shows a confection decked with tulips that carries no client associations. However, when the house participated in the 1948–49 Gratitude Train historical-figure series, this sketch was given credentials as an 1865 gown ordered by the Empress (figs. 1.100, 1.101). For the miniaturized version Worth fabricated the dress, Lesage contributed the embroidery, and Gabriel Fau coiffed the figure.

Later in the century a similar imperial respect for Worth's talent and judgment was shown by Marie Feodorovna, empress of Russia.[34] Worth senior reflected on this trust shortly before his death:

> Those ladies are wisest who leave the choice to us. By doing so they are always better pleased in the end, and the reputation of the house is sustained. Curiously enough, the persons who realize this fact most clearly are precisely those whom you might fancy the most difficult to please. For example, a telegram came from the Empress of Russia, "Send me a dinner dress!" Nothing more. We are left absolute freedom as to style and material. Not that the Empress is indifferent in the matter of dress. Quite the contrary. She will sometimes require that all the ladies' costumes at a certain ball be pink, or red, or blue. And her own dresses are always masterpieces of elegance. The point is she trusts our judgment rather than her own.[35]

For over thirty years Marie Feodorovna patronized Worth, under the guidance of both Charles Frederick and his sons, and by them was dressed in simple day and official court dress. In 1883, as a taste of summer during the Russian winter, she had a reception dress and train concocted of pink ottoman (looking like terry velvet) with trim of pink tulle and feathers, gold embroidery, and two thick garlands of velvet red roses and leaves. Her ball gown had a skirt of flounced pearl white tulle and orange velvet stripes trimmed with a profusion of nasturtiums and white flowers, according to one account, and daisies and buttercups, according to the other. These flowers

1.97, 1.98 Mrs. Cyrus Hall McCormick (née Nancy Maria [Nettie] Fowler) in her "hortensia" (hydrangea blue) silk-satin damask dress that was made c. 1903. Her photograph dates to c. 1904. Chicago Historical Society. (Photograph, Gift of Mrs. Howard Lin, 1954.228; dress, Gift of Mrs. Gilbert V. A. Harrison, 1954.288.)

1.99 (*Above*) House of Worth watercolor sketch, c. 1865, for the tulip-trimmed gown associated with Empress Eugénie. Present location unknown.

1.100 (*Above right*) Mannequin dressed in tulip-trimmed gown associated with Empress Eugénie. Photographed at Maison Worth with the portrait of Charles F. Worth in the background, 1948.

1.101 House of Worth watercolor sketch, c. 1948, for the mannequin's tulip-trimmed gown associated with Empress Eugénie. Victoria and Albert Museum E22207-1957.

detailed the bodice and train of orange-colored velvet.[36] The Empress's coronation attire included a Worth court train covered with dazzling embroidery in real silver over which needlewomen are said to have labored night and day for six weeks.

Other major royal patrons included Elizabeth, empress of Austria and queen of Hungary; Louisa, queen of Sweden; Margherita, princess of

Usedom; Maria Cristina, queen of Spain (who is said to have introduced a Worth-designed court manteau in 1879); and, finally, Ranavalona, queen of Madagascar, who on receiving a gift of Worth gowns and crinolines proceeded to wear one of the dresses but fabricated a tree canopy with its skirt supporter.[37] Even for queens, a toilette by Worth did not preclude derision. In late 1882 or early 1883, Italy's pretty Queen Margherita was observed at a court ball dressed in "orange colored satin, with a scarf of salmon-colored satin and panniers of black brocade, embroidered in colored flowers—a dress most unbecoming to the Queen, who is as fair as a Saxon girl, but which would suit a handsome, dark woman of matronly proportions."[38] Earlier, in 1879, it was noted she was dressed in exquisite simplicity—"simplicity, it is true, is not the fashion"—in a white princess-cut outfit. "She, even in winter, favored white while the ladies around her, however, prefer brighter colors. Ruby, red, yellow, orange and amber are among their favorite hues. Knowing this taste for showy colors Worth combines his dresses for his Italian customers accordingly, and thus, though a variety of colors is at times combined in one dress they are so combined that they always harmonize."[39] As a seventeen-year-old bride-to-be in 1866–67, Princess Margherita of Usedom was already wearing Worths. Walburga, Lady Paget, writes of an episode involving the young princess: "One day when coming into her room I found the whole place littered with lace and cherry colored bows, whilst she, with a big pair of scissors, was ripping off the trimming from a lovely grey silk dress, which had just arrived from Paris, one of Worth's choicest creations, and she explained to me that she simply did not like it and so she was pulling it to pieces. Anyone who can remember the prestige which surrounded Worth's name at that epoch must respect such independence."[40] Lady Paget penned her remarks in 1882–83, nearly twenty years later, when she found Worth still at the summit. In the 1920s Jean-Philippe Worth stated that at one point the house's only Italian client was Queen Margherita,[41] a fact that even he contradicts by saying other Italian aristocrats sought out the house. The 1884 wedding trousseau of Maria Massimo on her marriage to Prospero Colonna was made chiefly by Worth.

Continuing the patronage by Portuguese royal family members so auspiciously and adroitly begun by Queen Donna Maria da Gloria, queen regnant, in the early days of the house was Victor Emmanuel of Italy's daughter—who, as Queen Maria Pia, came to Jean-Philippe. He has written of her that nothing was ever too beautiful, too luxurious, or too expensive. Her patronage was followed briefly by that of Queen Amelia, daughter of the duchess of Galiera.

Of Spain's Bourbon monarchs, Jean-Philippe claimed five successive queens had been either direct or indirect clients. Queens Cristina, Isabella, Mercedes, Cristina (fig. 1.102), and Victoria and her daughter all wore Worths

1.102   Worth costumes in black and white, as seen on the cover of *Harper's Bazar*, July 23, 1892. The right model designed for Queen Cristina of Spain was of black faille covered with black embroidered net. Sketch by A. Sandoz.

Maison Rouff label easily confused with Worth
signature label
Woven garnet on white petersham
1890s

for official and unofficial functions. The second Queen Cristina had gone to the altar as the second wife of Alfonso XII in a wedding dress made, but not fitted, by Jean-Philippe. And the last queen, Victoria, was compelled by political pressure to buy at least part of her wardrobe in Madrid. She, therefore, favored dress shops that carried imported Worth models.

From 1882 we have descriptions of two gowns destined to appear at a midwinter court in Madrid. One, for Mme Valera, was of coralline velvet, with a train ruched with pink crepe lace in which were embedded enormous roses of the variety known as Princess Mary of Cambridge; the leaves were burnished a brown hue. Roses also crossed the bodice. A similarly trimmed dress had a tablier of silver brocade and a bodice of gold brocade with a waist-supported court train of pale blue brocade, studded with large gold flowers and bordered with an enormous pale blue crepe ruche in which were nestled yellowish green velvet rose leaves.[42]

In a sweeping and disdainful statement, Charles Frederick Worth reflected that his own monarch had ignored him: "We have worked for all the Courts, but never for Queen Victoria."[43] The queen had seen both the 1851 and 1855 exhibitions featuring entries by the fledgling designer, but she went into perpetual mourning when her beloved consort, Albert, died in 1861, just as Worth was establishing himself. She professed a preference for British products, moreover, but because of Worth's merchandising techniques, his models and/or his adaptations could well have found their way unofficially into Her Majesty's wardrobe. Jean-Philippe recalled making many dresses to Victoria's almost uniquely sizable measurements—which purveyors to the queen then imported. Great satisfaction was had on the rue de la Paix as the dressmaking establishment had the "joy of watching her complacently wearing [a Worth], believing it was untainted by alien handiwork."[44] British royals of the succeeding generation—Victoria's daughters and daughters-in-law—are known to have patronized Worth, sometimes openly, sometimes through intermediaries. Princess Helen of Waldeck-Prymont, for her marriage in 1882 to Queen Victoria's youngest son, Prince Leopold, duke of Albany, had her trousseau made in both London and Paris. The list of contributing English dressmakers is lengthy but one Parisian is listed: Worth. Alexandra, princess of Wales (later queen of Great Britain and Ireland), is documented as wearing Worths: in 1883 she had a "pretty dinner gown" of cream satin trimmed with narrow flounces of Brussels lace; the panniers were ornamented with plush appliqués, while the bodice and train were of pale claret velvet, the latter turned back with revers to match the pannier.[45] In 1882 Mme Tussaud's commissioned what was described as a "superb court toilette destined for the wax figure of the Princess of Wales. It consisted of a pale blue satin skirt, bordered with large clusters of plaits, fastened with a bow at the knee; the tablier is framed with a galoon sparkling with steel stars; bodice and train of blue damask, the design being hyacinths; the train bordered with a wide ruche of blue crepe and bouquets of tea roses; low bodice trimmed with blue crepe and silver fringe; for sleeves the flirting steel galoon, and the silver fringe."[46] In 1901 Alexandra commissioned her friend Mary, Lady Curzon—daughter of former dry-goods merchant Levi Zeigler Leiter, and wife of the Indian viceroy—to order needlework for her coronation robes and three other dresses. The handiwork, supervised by Mary, was executed in Darjeeling in February 1902. Perhaps at least one was made up by Worth, as was Mary's own viceregal gown a year later. Apparently, like her mother-in-law (but not like her sister, Dagmar, who became wife of Czar Alexander III), Alexandra was not a favorite with Jean-Philippe Worth. Though she was credited by many as being one of the most elegant and perpetually youthful personalities of her time, he saw her as "something of a dowd—she had the faculty of making any frock, no matter how smart or fresh or new, seem just another old rag."[47] He claims that only one dress was ever made for her; that it had been ordered by Lady de Grey, in a year not recalled, and fitted in-house because she came for fittings herself instead of trusting this detailed step to models.

English dress-making establishment active 1880s–1890s

In 1892 Lucy Hooper remarked that "there is scarcely a princess married in all of Europe—outside of the ladies of the Imperial family of Germany [who were relatives of the British royal family] whose principles forbid them from ever ordering anything to be made in Paris—that does not have a group of Worth toilettes included in her trousseau."[48] One who married into this exalted family wearing a Worth gown was Augusta Victoria Amelia Louise Marie Constance, eldest daughter of the grand duke and duchess of Schleswig-Holstein-Augustinburg, who was married on February 27, 1881, to Prince William of Prussia (Frederick William Victor Albert). For this royal wedding, which took place in Berlin, Worth made many of the dresses, including the beautiful white satin robe, *en tablier*, trimmed with fine silver and Honiton lace, with a long train of silver brocade. "Also some rich toilettes made of a new material manufactured especially for M. Worth, it is double-face satin of a delicate tender shade, called 'rayon de lune,' on one side and on the other known as 'crevette.'"[49] The lucky bride had one memorable dress of this fabric with a "pointed tablier of the material, the border being crevette, and the whole dress . . . bordered with an embroidery of pearls on net, the train was antique damask, a pale sea green ground covered with water lilies, the back of the bodice was damask, the front of the lune and 'crevette' satin."[50] Jean-Philippe partially contradicts the Hooper statement on imperial Germanic consideration of Parisian modes as sources of contraband.[51] Worth creations were frequently obtained indirectly by prominent personages who officially endorsed domestic products and industries. Thus, models were sold to Berlin dressmakers, who merchandised the garments first

Woven gold on black WORTH/New York Frame surmounted by: "No Connection With Any (Shield) Foreign Establishment" c. 1900–20

1.103 Princess Hélène in her court-presentation attire as fabricated by Worth in 1892/93.

1.104 Worth toilette for Princess Mathilde, as documented in *L'Art et la mode*, Sept. 1888. For court wear, the princess appeared in a bodice and train of floral-brocaded silk-satin ground. Her underskirt was draped with gray tulle ornamented with pearls.

to Empress Augusta, wife of Wilhelm I, and later to her daughter-in-law, Queen Victoria's daughter, Princess Victoria of Prussia. She became a client before her husband's accession, and it is believed her wardrobe contained garments sold directly to her from Paris and some acquired through more public channels.

Owing to her connections with the German royal family, Sophia, queen to Oskar II of Sweden, reportedly did not follow Queen Louisa in her patronage of Worth. Ascending to the throne in 1873, she no longer felt obligated to encourage the firm from which her countryman, Otto Bobergh, was now separated.

Elizabeth, empress of Austria and queen of Hungary, as elegant and with as troubled a life as her contemporary Eugénie, apparently never graced the salons of Worth but rather would order several gowns each year, to be made up in simplified styles in rich stuffs of the white-pearl, gray, and palest violet shades.

Those surrounding the crowned heads—court and its select society—also sought out Worth's talents. The heyday of confecting couture for court had come during the Second Empire. To two Austrians go the honors of showcasing Worth's designs. The self-acknowledgedly less than pretty Princess Pauline von Metternich (née Pauline Sandor de Szlavnicza; 1836–1921), wife of the Austrian ambassador to the French imperial court and great favorite with all at court, is generally acknowledged as making the initial introduction. A trendsetter, she is later credited with wearing Worth's first short walking costume to the races, where so many future fashions would be introduced. Through a judicious bit of sleuthing, Diana de Marly has been able to match up a photograph of the princess in one of her Worth dresses with one of the house sketches.[52] Princess Pauline's influence outlasted the fall of the Second Empire, and her patronage of Worth remained strong. In 1881 she ordered what was described as "a rich toilette . . . of magnificent satin—white ground studded all over with large bouquets of shaded red carnations"[53] with an extremely long, plain undraped train. The second Austrian client of reputation, a cousin of the French emperor, was Princess Mathilde (fig. 1.104). She had a most European international background—a Corsican father, German mother, Russian husband (Prince Demidoff), and a Dutch lover. Born in Austria, she was brought up in Italy and lived in France. Her dedication to Worth lasted her lifetime.

Virginia Oldalin (b. before 1822, d. 1902), the most talked-about woman of the 1860s, who gained fame as an international Second Empire beauty as Contessa Castiglione, was another client. Lillie Moulton remembered that *Figaro* considered this Italian—even during her days of greatest notoriety, when she was well into her forties—a classic beauty, but entirely without charm. At the time of her death, the mirrors in her home on the place

Vendôme were "covered with black stuff of some kind; she did not wish to see the sad relics of her beauty. . . . Her things were sold at auction—piles of old ball shoes, headgear, gloves stiffened with moisture and age."[54] She was always so extraordinarily dressed that she invariably created a sensation.

Other ladies of the French imperial court and members of their families parading in Worths included Comtesse de Pourtales, Duchesse de Morny (née Princess Troubebtskoy), Princess Anna Murat (late Duchesse de Mouchy). These were followed by Comtesse de Beauharnais, whose square-trained ball dress of cream satin and tulle with garlands of dark pansies mixed with silver lilies of the valley was one of the most beautiful dresses of the 1882–83 holiday season; Princess Hélène d'Orléans, who had a court dress and mantel in 1892/93 (fig. 1.103); and Comtesse de Noailles. For Elisabeth de Caraman-Chimay, comtesse Greffulhe, there were two breathtakingly beautiful gowns, both in the Musée de la Mode et du Costume, Paris: a black velvet evening dress encrusted with pearls, outlining appliqués of cream satin in a bold lily motif (figs. 1.105, 1.106); and her 1902 mother-of-the-bride silvery gray encrusted reception dress (Musée de la Mode et du Costume, Paris, 78.20.2). Also in this collection are several garments from the wardrobe of Princess Murat (née Cécile Ney d'Elchingen, 61.65.1).

Because so many of England's ladies of title were American heiresses, or "dollar princesses," it is a complex matter to ascertain the origin of their association with Worth. Lady Randolph Churchill, formerly Jennie Jerome of New York City, had spent years of her youth in Paris. Vanderbilt family women long patronized Worth; it was only natural that the family swan, Consuelo, duchess of Marlborough, should have a sea blue satin evening dress whose train was trimmed with white ostrich feathers, a pink velvet gown decorated with sables, and a 1905 white satin dress brocaded with flowers outlined with diamonds.

In 1895 Worth made a wedding dress for Mary Victoria Leiter, on her marriage to George Nathaniel Curzon, later Viscount Scarsdale. "Simplicity itself," said the *Chicago Tribune* of the white satin gown trimmed with old lace and a full train, meaning that Worth had worked on it for weeks.[55] For her investiture as vicerine of India in 1903, Lady Curzon continued her interest in encouraging native Indian crafts: as done previously for less formal garments, she had the stunning metal embroidery in a peacock-feather motif locally stitched but had the gown itself fashioned by Worth (fig. 1.107). The eyes of the feathers were highlighted with bright blue-and-green beetle wings—not real emeralds, so some claimed.

The consensus among Worth clients was that their toilettes were worth the expense because of the consternation they caused among rivals. While Walburga, Lady Paget, was visiting Berlin between 1860 and 1863, Annie de Moltke sent her a gift of some Worth garments, which she wore in the

1.105, 1.106 Jean-Philippe Worth is said to have created this black silk-velvet evening gown appliquéd with pearl-and-gilt-beaded ivory-satin lilies for the memorable Elisabeth de Caraman-Chimay, comtesse Greffulhe. The inspiration for Proust's Duchesse de Guermantes, this lovely lady was captured by the camera of Paul Nadar in 1896. She struck two poses, which can be differentiated by the displacement of her collar. The gown is preserved in the Musée de la Mode et du Costume, Paris. Nadar Archives, inv. nos. 4026, 4027.

1.107 As the wife of George Curzon, Lord Scarsdale the Viceroy of India, the beautiful and accomplished Mary Leiter of Chicago was in a position to encourage native crafts. A brilliant example is her 1902 ceremonial gown embroidered in colored metallic threads in an ocean of peacock-feather-eye tips. Embroidery skills of India were mated with Worth design in this garment.

1.108 "Elegant dress, made . . . for a stately English Duchess" of dark steel gray peau de soie trimmed with old-silver passementerie. Created to be worn to the races, it appeared on the cover of the May 28, 1892, issue of *Harper's Bazar*.

presence of Countess Lory Wittgenstein, who Lady Paget says was "plain, but had a splendid figure, and was more chic than anybody I had ever met. She was most patronizing to me about my clothes." Then came the Worth "works of art," and nothing more was said.[56] At one 1870s event at Epsom, the English horse race, Lady Sykes "appeared in a dress even too gorgeous for a ball! An embroidered princess gown, worked as exquisitely as any Louis XV dress, with a train two meters [over six feet] long"—just the thing for cutting a track of your own at a crowded event.[57]

Of the Russian aristocracy, at least two morganatic wives, Mlle Youriwitch, wife to Alexander II, and Princess Paley, presented at court as Countess Hohen Felsen but wife to Grand Duke Paul, were regally attired by the house. Princess Bariatinski and her two daughters chose to shop at Worth. One daughter was the extravagant Countess Sophia Paul Chauvaloff, who later married Count Beckendorff, an ambassador to London. Her splendid court-presentation ensemble of satins was enriched with metallic threads and freshwater pearls (fig. 1.109).

The extravagance associated with a Worth would put some aristocratic clients on edge and the position as a domestic servant on the line. Once princess von Metternich complained to her hostess, Melanie, comtesse de

1.109 Court-presentation trained gown in the Russian style encrusted with freshwater pearls, c. 1890, as fashioned by Worth for the spendthrift Countess Beckendorff, wife of Count Alexander Konstantinovitch Beckendorff, Russian ambassador to the Court of Saint James's. Wadsworth Atheneum, Hartford, Gift of Elizabeth Hicks, 1962.459.

Portalès, that her clumsy lackey had just abused her superb evening cloak, fresh from the hands of Worth by rolling it up like the commonest mantle.[58] In October 1877 Walburga, Lady Paget, wrote: "I've had to tell Mrs. Hurly she must depart. . . . I found one of my best Worth dresses shoved in to a window on the servants' staircase at Heron Court, with my shoes thrown on top."[59]

The establishment of the Third Republic did not reduce Worth's clientele in France. Much has been written about the excesses and misdirected values of the Second Empire, but even the coup d'état in 1870 barely lessened the need of parvenus and international adventurers to bolster their newfound status. They lavished fortunes on outward luxury; as the actress-courtesan and Worth client Cora Pearl observed, "Vice is seldom clad in rags." Even the wives of the presidents of the Republic of France found temptation irresistible, and three out of four Mmes Thiers, MacMahon, and Carnot succumbed to fripperies from Worth. Mme Thiers (née Dosne) had been a beauty in her youth, which aided her in overcoming some of the bourgeois aspects of her husband's tenure. She appeared at state functions attired in embroidered black gowns designed by Worth to set off her well-known pearl necklace.

1.110 (*Opposite*) Sarah Bernhardt in *Fédora*, wearing a blue-green gown strewn with violet blossoms. As sketched by Mars in *L'Art et la mode*, Dec. 1883.

1.111, 1.112 This "simple" at-home dress, designed by Worth for Sarah Bernhardt to wear in the second act of *Fédora*, was altered by the actress for each performance. Sketched by Mars for *L'Art et la mode*, Nov. 1883 and Dec. 1883.

Idiosyncratic clients from all levels of society brought their demands to Worth, knowing that even the most outrageous request would receive consideration. One of the more demanding clients from the Second Empire period was Señora Erazu from Mexico, who one day announced that she had taken a vow never to wear silk again, only brown wool. But she was to have ball and dinner dresses, day outfits, everything in her prescribed cloth of penance; she was a very regular customer, ordering, it is said, at least two new dresses a week. Another single-color client was Walburga, Lady Paget, who favored white because she "suffered from inharmonious colors." In 1882 she would write: "It is the famous Worth's 'grief' against me that I will never order any but white dresses. 'Toujours ces robes blanches,' he says, but I am still one of his favored clients."[60]

While Doucet was far more active in dressing stage actresses, both in and out of role, a fair number sought out Worth for both their ordinary attire and their contemporary or historical outfits for the stage. (Historical and other stage wear are not considered in this publication.) The house valued its association with actresses—from Cora Pearl and the Italian Adelaide Ristori (star of the Odéon), at the beginning, to Eleanora Duse, through the final days of Jean-Philippe. As the junior Worth said: "The theatre is one of the most active agents in the propagation of fashion. By her personal charm a popular and graceful actress may contribute to the adoption of an ordinary idea."[61] This statement was made in reference to the "Manteau de chambre," a long, fitted indoor coat not unlike an academic gown, which had been devised for Duse in about 1903 and immediately became a house staple. In Edith Wharton's novel *The Age of Innocence*, Mrs. Baxter Pennilow and other women of similarly refined breeding put away their newest gowns for a season or two because only actresses and their like went about in such ostentation.

Marie Louise Marsy of the Comédie Française appeared in the 1890 production *Une Famille* in several characteristic Worth fashionable garments, one having an almost house-signature texture pattern of a fish-scale design and the other incorporating a large leaf motif. Both garments enforced her leading-lady, not ingenue, status.

The Australian opera singer Nellie Melba compliments Jean-Philippe for "making me realize how important it was to look as well as I sang . . . some garments were dreams of beauty . . . I always felt very smart when I came back from Paris with a new collection of Worth dresses, although when I look at the rather faded photographs of myself in those days I can hardly help laughing at the fantastic fashions we used to think beautiful."[62] She had, on her initial arrival in Paris in 1886, but one winter dress, which was continually worn to the frustration of her voice teacher, Mme Marchesi, who implored Melba to "Run to Worth's now and buy yourself the most beautiful

1.113, 1.114 Lillie Langtry was twice captured languishing in Worth gowns. The c. 1888 image by Lafayette of London shows her in a seventeenth-century-style evening gown. The later photograph, of c. 1900, shows her wearing a gown of velvet-patterned silk satin, which can be related to Worth fabric in extant garments.

dress you can find. I pay. I pay.''[63] Jean-Philippe Worth, however, says in his memoir that Melba was introduced to the house by a Belgian friend.[64]

Several years earlier, in 1882–83, Worth had been invited at the last minute to participate in dressing the rail-thin Sarah Bernhardt for her role in Sardou's *Fédora* (figs. 1.110–1.112). The play was one of the greatest triumphs of the "divine Sarah," and her wardrobe received considerable press. Although the enthusiastic critics proclaimed that soon the world would be dressed *à la Fédora*, the collaboration was by accounts a first and final association. Worth was asked to design two garments but convinced Sarah he should do all five, one for each act—three ball, one day, and one "deshabille." On opening night, with Worth in attendance, Sarah wore only two, infuriating the designer. He was not willing to share dressmaker billing with Mme Morin, whose failure to satisfy Sarah initially had driven the actress to Worth, Felix, and others. A bill was rendered demanding payment and threatening attachment of salary. A war was on. Each evening Sarah had the garments slightly altered, so that she seemed never to appear in the same gown twice. Fiddling with the master's designs could not have further endeared her to Worth. One can see the minor changes she executed from sketches of the "deshabille," where she added fichu and drape to cover some of the rows of lace flounces. The gowns were described as full of beauty and simplicity, although the latter quality is hardly conceivable, given the cascades of lace, flowers, and beaded trim. The pearls alone on one Worth garment were said to be valued at Fr 100,000.[65]

Emily Charlotte le Breton—better known by her stage name, Lillie Langtry—acquired much of both her personal and her professional wardrobe (from at least 1885 on) from Worth (figs. 1.113, 1.114). She reputedly tried to negotiate her bill by promising a North American tour with advertisements in every program.[66] Surely the Worths saw the ploy only as icing on their American cake. After her marriage to Hugo de Bathe, Lillie's patronage declined.

Other theatrical and concert personalities attended to by Worth included the American opera star Emma Eames (see fig. 1.52), whose garments, inspired by historical documents, were particularly well received and many of which are preserved in the collection of the Museum of the City of New York. The Swedish singer Christine Nilsson was introduced to the house by Bobergh, and over the years she sang at the Théâtre Lyrique in many Worth outfits (fig. 1.115). Worth was exclusive couturier to Adelina Patti, who became a valued client and family friend, and to her singing friend Mme Albani (later Mrs. Gye). The Brohan sisters Augustine and Madeleine (the latter a great beauty, notwithstanding an inclination to stoutness) and Mme Bartet, all of the Comédie Française, came to Worth for both stage and contemporary clothes, as did Sybil Sanderson, who ordered a few costumes and all her town clothes. Mme Rosa Caron, however, only had her private dress clothes from the house.

A review of Worth's clientele would not be complete without mention of absentee clients, to whom Jean-Philippe referred in 1896: "One curious development of modern life is that so many people order their clothes in Paris who have perhaps never been within sight of France. People write to us from all over America. We often send photographs of some of our newest creations to all parts of the world."[67] By 1897 communications with the house were expedited by the installation of a telephone.

Clients, great or unremembered, clung to the name Worth, many remaining lifelong patrons. The fin de siècle was an age of aspirations, and while most wore their many Worths in almost fairy-tale existences, others, owning one cherished gown, aimed at a brief moment of showering stardust. Whether the following story from the 1890s is apocryphal or satirical, it is leavening counterpoint to the pomp surrounding most Worth garments:

> A man who has been travelling through some newly discovered oil fields tells the story of finding in a farmhouse, whose owner had just struck oil, a handsome girl in full evening costume beating madly on the keys of a grand piano. The only deficiency in her toilette, to a casual observer, was the fact that she wore neither shoes nor stockings. When asked to explain this she seemed greatly surprised and said that pa had told her that everybody who was rich always bought a dress from Mr. Worth and a big grand piano. But "pa" had evidently not read of shoes or stockings![68]

1.115 The concert artist Christine Nilsson, in a Worth toilette of French faille with Persian flowers embroidered in metallic threads. As seen in *L'Art et la mode*, May 16, 1885.

APPENDIX

Worth Labels

House labels are arranged chronologically in the text and are augmented with spurious and related examples.

Not all the visual evidence for authenticating a Worth garment is to be found on the exterior. It was sometime during the earliest years of the 1860s that the House of Worth and Bobergh began identifying their garments by stamping the interior waistband, a sewn-in inner belt, which would in time be identified as a "petersham." Whether this house was the first dressmaking

Summer (Eté) or Winter (Hiver) collection
stamp, in blue
1897

establishment to identify its creations is not known, but the procedure of attaching an impression of at least a name and a city into a garment was adopted at this time. As with the fashions that bore the markings, there were both subtle and extreme changes in the schematics of labels. During the period of the Franco-Prussian war and the Siege of Paris, the name Bobergh disappeared from the early gold-stamped labels (see pp. 9, 19).[1]

Worth garments of the 1880s seem to carry three house-generated petersham labels, the earliest being the printed gold on white carried over from the previous decade (see p. 20). (It was late in the decade of the eighties that the first spurious Worth label seems to have been generated.) For outerwear items the label was introduced as a gold stamp on black. The middle years of the decade, beginning in 1883–84, seem to be identified by the most uncomplicated of all genuine Worth labels—"Worth" over "Paris"—in an elliptical form (see p. 27). Worked in white on white, this version is usually found in dresses and gowns, and in black on black in outerwear. The application of this version was very short-lived, possibly lasting only three or four years. Sometime near the end of the decade came the changeover to the "Charles Worth" signature label (see p. 31), a trademark that would, in several woven versions, continue until the house's demise. For the first two decades of its application, the format did not change, just the length and depth of the configuration of "Paris—C Worth—Paris" and the width of the woven petersham band. Initially the signature was woven in shades of dark brown silk so that on the label face the name takes on a silvery-gold appearance.[2] However, study has revealed that even the signature label changed almost imperceptibly, shrinking both vertically and horizontally over time. There seems to be no clear line of demarcation as to when a label of one dimension was replaced by another. Broadly speaking, signature labels run between 18.2 centimeters and, at the outside, 20 centimeters, and identify garments made before 1894. Thereafter, most labels range between 16.4 centimeters and 17.4 centimeters, although a few reach 18.2 centimeters.[3]

For wraps and accessories the central signature was extracted and used alone, appearing first in brown woven with white and presenting the silvery-gold appearance, and later in gold with black (see p. 34).[4] After about 1900 a white-on-white signature label was introduced for outerwear; these smaller labels were generally located in the center-back neckline area (see p. 51).

One of the difficulties of making any hard-and-fast proclamations about the precise date of a garment without additional substantiating evidence is demonstrated by two evening garments of about 1880 held by the Museum of the City of New York (31.3.4, 38.220.12). These ball gowns are confected from different colorways of the same fabric, with a large stalked dahlia blossom, but each carries a very different Worth label: one the gold-stamped version of about 1871 to about 1884; and the other, the later trademark signature woven in brown silk on white (see pp. 20, 31). This second label, from stitching evidence, is not original to the garment. Did the bodice originally carry the presumed proper identifying label, and did the owner, a known Worth client, in an old, established pursuit, merely move labels around? In another instance the two bodices for a three-piece 1893–94 ensemble bear signature labels of two different dimensions (pls. 10–11). It has been assumed that the bodices were fabricated contemporaneously. Perhaps the bodice with the larger label was fitted earlier for it carries an older stock label, possibly the result of seamstresses drawing from the ream of labels closest to hand. Also unknown is whether there was only one supplier of labels to Worth at any given time. Multiple suppliers would help explain some of the minor discrepancies in scale that one finds within the chronology of the labels.

Confirming the author's assumptions, nearly half of the garments examined for this project from the 1880s boast the signature label (see p. 31). But among the genuine labels of the 1880s there lurk several suspicious specimens in which neither the quality and cast of the label nor the garment to which it is attached have an authentic air (see pp. 84, 85, 88, 89).[5]

The year 1897 is a pivotal one because a blue rubber-stamp impression was applied to the petersham (see p. 108). It identified products made during the winter and summer collection season; garments designed or made during the demi-seasons are not so marked. The marking is square, bordered on three sides. The top band carries "Paris", with the right side a decorative line; the bottom band has the season and year. At the center is a stylized, leftward-facing androgynous bust with long, flowing tresses. Because Gaston Worth was at this time organizing the Chambre Syndicale de la Haute Couture Française, it is possible that this stamp was a trial method of further identifying genuine articles of French manufacture as opposed to authorized or pirated copies. However, the value of these stamps extends far beyond their importance in accurately dating particular garments: in conjunction with the five-digit house order numbers, which are concealed on the back of the petersham bands, the stamps also make it possible to conjecture when other garments might have been made. Up to about 1904, most of these five-digit numbers were handwritten in ink on linen or cotton tape and stitched to the petersham.[6] There are two sets of numbers: one for outer wraps (coats, pelerines, jackets, capes, collets, tailored suits) and a second series for dresses, gowns and at-home wear. Purple rubber-stamp impressions first appear on the tapes in wraps and are used in all garments from about 1906.

More than three hundred Worth garments that could be dated between 1894 and 1905 have been examined by the author. Of this group, two-thirds bore numbered tags. In several instances consecutive or near-consecutive numbers were documented, and these can be associated with a specific client, on a shopping spree or wardrobe renewal.[7] The numbering sequence for outerwear and tailored garments begins with *1*, *2*, or *3*, while *4* through *9* are reserved for all other garments.

The earliest year to which garments tagged with these numbers have been traced is 1894. Using the numbers attached to the dated 1897 dresses as a base and working back from selected model numbers in the Worth photographic archives, the author proposes 1887, when business advanced following several economically unstable years, as the year that the system began.

Jean-Philippe's production claims for the most active years of the house—an average of 5,000 orders per year—are corroborated by the following chart correlating years and model numbers for dresses, if the 5,000 figure is taken to include couture work, export models, refittings, and restylings. It should be borne in mind that some garments—such as wedding dresses and court-presentation gowns—that have a specific date associated with them could actually have been ordered in a preceding year.

DRESSES AND GOWNS

Year	Model Numbers	Year	Model Numbers
1887	10000–44000	1897	89000–94000
1888	44000–49000	1898	94000–100000
1889	49000–54000	1899	40000–46000
1890	54000–59000	1900	46000–52000
1891	59000–64000	1901	52000–57000
1892	64000–69000	1902	57000–62000
1893	69000–74000	1903	62000–67000
1894	74000–79000	1904	67000–71000
1895	79000–84000	1905	71000–75000
1896	84000–89000	1906	75000–79000
		1907	79000–[8]

Interpretation of the tailored-garment categories is not as easily accomplished. As revealed in the photographic archive books, the earliest of these have been dated to 1889. The numbering system begins with *1* for wraps and *2* for suits. (Outerwear jackets inconsistently cross over numbering systems.) Some suits are in an album dated 1900–03, but it appears that numbering them separately began only in 1901. A rough guide for suits can be offered.

SUITS

Year	Model Numbers	Year	Model Numbers
1901	20000–21000	1904	23400–24800
1902	21000–22200	1905	24800–27000
1903	22200–23400	1906	27000–29800
		1907	29800–

Some confusion results from the fact that suit and wrap numbers are intermingled on the usually purple-stamped tapes. The following is a guide to the archival numbered coats, wraps, pelerines, and other outerwear.

OUTERWEAR

Year	*Model Numbers*
1899–1900	10000–11600
1900–1901	11600–13100
1901–1902	13100–14600
1902–1903	14600–15100
1903–1904	15100–16600
1904–1905	16600–18100
1905–1906	18100–19600
1906–1907	10000–11600
1907–	11600–

Because numbers beginning with *3* do not appear in the archival books and because less than a dozen chronologically widely spaced items were examined within this series, no hypotheses can be offered on a dating guide. All items numbered with *3* fell into the coat/suit tailored-garment category. A handsome midnight blue silk-velvet suit or outer jacket with Renaissance-style appliquéd motifs at the Philadelphia Museum of Art (74.86.1) is numbered 32568 and can be reasonably dated to about 1895–96, as it is pictured, with the addition of fur edging, in an issue of *Harper's Bazar* of 1895 (see fig. 1.34). Slightly earlier, from about 1893, is a redingote in an exuberant prickly-pear cactus-patch motif of cut black velvet, numbered 29756 (The Metropolitan Museum of Art, 50.1.6), and a tailored winter suit numbered 37558 (The Brooklyn Museum, 65.185.14) can be related to another *Harper's Bazar* cover image, from February 26, 1898. Additional attempts have been made to crack codes inscribed in the archival books.

❧❧❧❧❧❧❧

Plate 1   Charles F. Worth. *Afternoon Dress*, c. 1872. Chevron-patterned silk satin and faille. Worn by Alice Wells. The Brooklyn Museum, Gift of Alice Wells, 33.74

Plate 2   Charles F. Worth. *Debutante Dress*, c. 1882. Plain silk satin and tulle; artificial roses. Probably worn by Miss Eleanor Hewitt. The Brooklyn Museum, Gift of the Princess Viggo in accordance with the wishes of the Misses Hewitt, 31.31

Plate 3   Charles F. Worth. *Reception Dress*, c. 1880. Egyptian-motif-patterned silk damask; machine-embroidered net lace. The Brooklyn Museum, Gift of the Pierrepont Family, 41.319

Plate 4   Charles F. Worth. *Walking Dress*, c. 1885. Striped silk satin and faille; moiré ribbon and passementerie trim. The Brooklyn Museum, Gift of Mrs. C. M. Andrews, 51.61.4

Plate 5   Charles F. or Jean-Philippe Worth. *Evening Dress*, 1888. Elliptical-patterned silk-satin damask; silk velvet and cut-steel-bead trim. Probably worn by Mrs. Abram Hewitt or Miss Sarah Hewitt. The Brooklyn Museum, Gift of the Princess Viggo in accordance with the wishes of the Misses Hewitt, 31.24

Plate 6   Charles F. Worth. *Day Dress*, c. 1888. Striped silk moiré; mousseline de soie trim. The Brooklyn Museum, Gift of Mrs. William E. S. Griswold, 41.915

Plate 7   Charles F. or Jean-Philippe Worth. *Day Dress*, c. 1886. Silk faille patterned with stars; silk appliquéd with beaded braid. The Brooklyn Museum, Gift of Mrs. William E. S. Griswold, 41.913

Plate 8   Charles F. or Jean-Philippe Worth. *Sortie de Bal*, 1889. Silk lampas, "Tulipes Hollandaises" by MM. Gourd & Cie. Worn by one of the Misses Hewitt. The Brooklyn Museum, Gift of the Princess Viggo in accordance with the wishes of the Misses Hewitt, 31.22

Plate 9   Charles F. or Jean-Philippe Worth. *"Empire" Day Dress*, 1892. Wool and silk ottoman; machine lace and glass-bead trim. The Brooklyn Museum, Anonymous Gift in memory of Mrs. John Roebling, 70.53.6

Plate 10   Charles F. or Jean-Philippe Worth. *Dress with Dinner Bodice*, 1894. Silk satin patterned with chrysanthemum petals; silk velvet, machine lace, and cut-steel beads. Worn by Mrs. William Alfred Perry. The Brooklyn Museum, Gift of Edith V. Gardiner in memory of Mrs. William Alfred Perry, 26.372

Plate 11   Charles F. or Jean-Philippe Worth. *Dress with Evening Bodice*, 1894. Silk satin patterned with chrysanthemum petals; silk velvet and machine lace. Worn by Mrs. William Alfred Perry. The Brooklyn Museum, Gift of Edith V. Gardiner in memory of Mrs. William Alfred Perry, 26.372

Plate 12   Charles F. or Jean-Philippe Worth. *Winter Carriage Ensemble* (wrap, princess dress, muff, and Virot hat), 1894. Silk, patterned with cut and uncut pile; fur, jet-bead, and lace trim. Worn by Mrs. William Alfred Perry. The Brooklyn Museum, Gift of Edith V. Gardiner in memory of Mrs. William Alfred Perry, 26.358

Plate 13   Jean-Philippe Worth. *Seventeenth-century-style Reception Dress*, c. 1895. Silk crepe and satin; machine-made lace. Worn by one of the Misses Hewitt. The Brooklyn Museum, Gift of the Princess Viggo in accordance with the wishes of the Misses Hewitt, 31.65

Plate 14   Charles F. or Jean-Philippe Worth. *Ball Gown*, 1894. Silk patterned with feathers; silk velvet and appliquéd lace trim. Worn by Mrs. William Alfred Perry. The Brooklyn Museum, Gift of Miss Edith V. Gardiner in memory of Mrs. William Alfred Perry, 26.374

Plate 15   Jean-Philippe Worth. *Reception or Tea Gown*, 1894. Silk patterned with peacock feathers; silk satin and lace trim. Worn by one of the Misses Hewitt. The Brooklyn Museum, Gift of the Princess Viggo in accordance with the wishes of the Misses Hewitt, 31.47

Plate 16   Jean-Philippe Worth. *Evening Dress*, 1898. Silk taffeta warp-printed with cherries; mousseline de soie, ribbon, machine-made lace trim. Worn by a member of the Hewitt family. The Brooklyn Museum, Gift of the Princess Viggo in accordance with the wishes of the Misses Hewitt, 31.23

Plate 17   Jean-Philippe Worth. *Walking Suit*, 1898. Silk cut velvet, embroidered silk, machine-made lace, moiré ribbon trim. Probably worn by Miss Eleanor Hewitt. The Brooklyn Museum, Gift of the Princess Viggo in accordance with the wishes of the Misses Hewitt, 31.30

Plate 18   Jean-Philippe Worth. *Ball Gown*, 1900. Silk satin; embroidered with brilliants and beads in wheat-stalk motif; machine-made lace. The Brooklyn Museum, Gift of Mrs. C. Phillip Miller, 57.83.22

Plate 19   Jean-Philippe Worth. *Evening Coat*, 1900. Silk satin patterned with cut pile patterned in honeysuckle; mousseline de soie and embroidered net-lace trim. The Brooklyn Museum, Gift of Mrs. C. Oliver Iselin, 61.219.2

Plate 20   Jean-Philippe Worth. *Ball Gown*, 1898. Silk satin woven *en disposition* with butterflies; velvet ribbon, appliquéd net lace, glass beads, and brilliant trim. The Brooklyn Museum, Gift of Mrs. Paul G. Pennoyer, 65.189.2

Plate 21   Jean-Philippe Worth. *Late Day Dress*, 1900. Silk panne velvet appliquéd with wool broadcloth and silk cording in imitation of Venetian gros point lace; silk-satin ribbon trim. Worn by Mrs. William Alfred Perry. The Brooklyn Museum, Gift of Miss Edith V. Gardiner in memory of Mrs. William Alfred Perry, 26.380

Plate 22   Jean-Philippe Worth. *Evening Dress*, 1902. Silk taffeta warp-printed with roses; guipure lace and satin-ribbon trim. The Brooklyn Museum, Gift of Mrs. C. Oliver Iselin, 61.291.6

Plate 23   Jean-Philippe Worth. *Evening Mantle*, 1901. Silk voided velvet in ribbon-and-floral-garland pattern, sable collar. Worn by Mrs. Alfred William Perry. The Brooklyn Museum, Gift of Miss Edith V. Gardiner in memory of Mrs. William Alfred Perry, 26.375

Plate 24   Jean-Philippe Worth. *Evening Dress*, 1905. Silk panne velvet printed with roses; machine-made net lace, silk satin. The Brooklyn Museum, Gift of Mrs. C. Oliver Iselin, 61.219.5

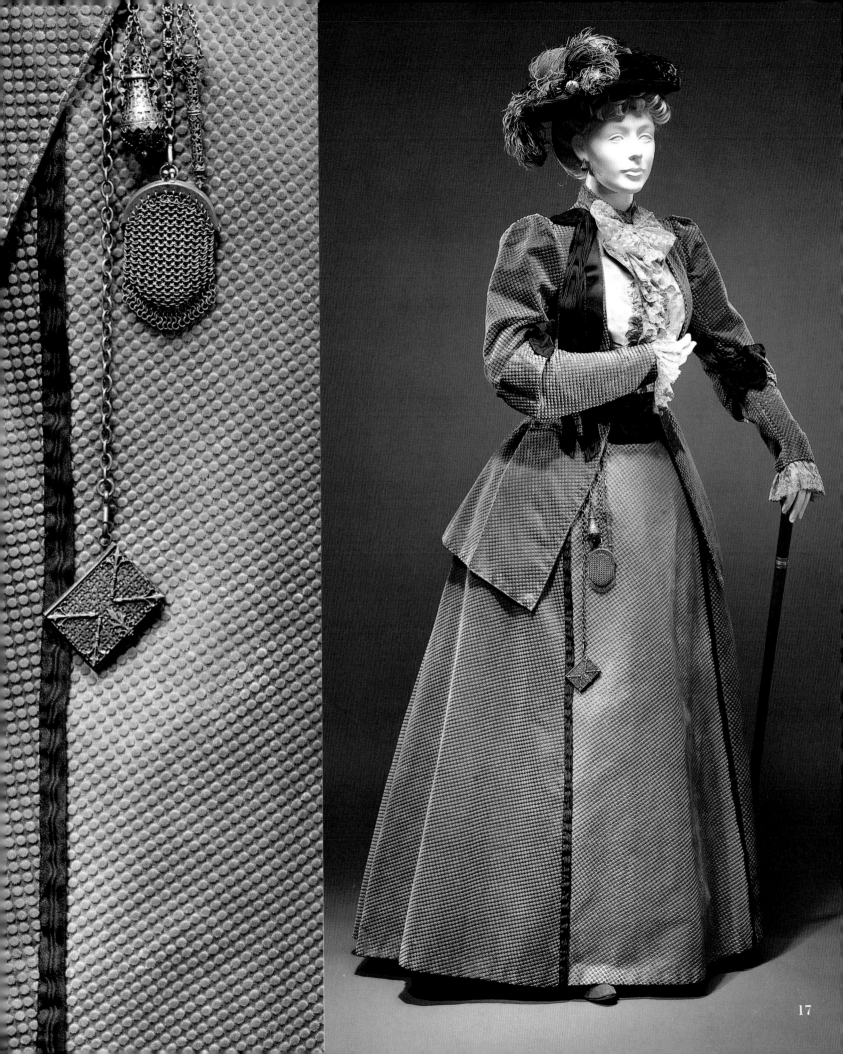

2
The House of Doucet

THE DOUCET FAMILY BUSINESSES

The House of Doucet, classified in 1915 as the oldest of all the *maisons de couture*,[1] rose to prominence in the world of women's fashion during the years that Jacques Doucet (1853–1929) headed the establishment. It was only in the early 1870s, however, not long after Jacques entered the business founded by his grandfather some fifty-five years before, that custom-made ladies' attire had become the primary focus of the house (fig. 2.1).

Indeed, generations of Doucets had found occupation with fabrics and the making of clothing for all ages and genders. As early as the 1840s, the house claimed to have been established in 1817, although the first listings for the name Doucet in conjunction with textiles do not appear in the Paris trade directories until 1822, when G. Doucet and Doucet et Cie are both listed as silk merchants at 11 Neuve des Petit Champs.[2] In other, secondary, sources the date of the founding of the firm varies from 1815 on. Some authors have the Doucets beginning as sellers of headwear decorated with lace and peddling their wares from a "porch in one of the busiest quarters in Paris."[3] Others write that Jacques's grandfather Antoine Doucet and his wife, cofounders of the firm, had a stall in 1816 on the boulevard Beaumarchais, where they specialized in laces. Antoine Doucet (1795–1866) is documented as embarking in business in 1824 at 25 boulevard Saint-Martin—then one of the best shopping streets in Paris—and making lingerie and fashionable items there in 1830. These various moves must be indicative of both shrewd business practices and commodities of increasing interest to the public. Financial backing in the form of a partnership with a M. Denion-Dupin was arranged in 1826; the Doucets supplied the talent and a third of the capital.[4] The directory listing shows that lingerie was clearly the major merchandising component: "assortim., considérable de broderies et de lingerie confectionnées, fab[ricant] de chemises en gros et en détail" (considerable assortment of embroideries, and ready-made lingerie, manufacturer of shirts in bulk and in

Stamped gold on white petersham
c. 1880–90

137

2.1   Jean Beraud (1849–1936), *La Devanture du
Couturier Doucet*, c. 1899. Mme M. Roche, Paris.

2.2 Artist's rendering of the façade of Maison Doucet, rue de la Paix, and listing of the various enterprises carried on within, c. 1850.

custom). Riding high on expanding business, the firm again relocated: by April 1840 the Doucets had taken a twenty-year lease on quarters at 17 rue de la Paix,[5] retaining the Saint-Martin address as a branch shop, which also included workrooms. In 1841 and 1857, the firm absorbed still more space at number 17. The move to the rue de la Paix signaled Antoine's understanding of the shifting locale for fashionable shopping, then clustering at the foot of the column of the place Vendôme. Already considered an established concern, Maison Doucet marked the passage of over twenty years in business by advertising that they had been the first to make a speciality of the art of linen accessories for men, having devised the shirt that incorporated a bib front; this shirt, with minor adaptations, is worn still, as formal attire.

A rendering of about 1850 (fig. 2.2) of the building's façade, used on both billheads and prospectus, may be misleading in its inclusion of the name Doucet all over the building, but from this address the Doucets did manage several interrelated businesses. The operation did not confine itself to masculine haberdashery, but offered other lingerie items and embroidered works, laces, trousseau objects, and layettes. Specialities in 1840 included tailored shirts, waisted drawers, and flannel waistcoats, to which are added in 1845 braces (suspenders), hosiery, collars, and gloves. They even provided maintenance services, doing laundry and pressing on the premises.

139

2.3 Fashion illustration sketched by Numa and published in *La Mode*, Aug. 9, 1841, depicting chemise and voile by Doucet for a riding costume.

Other random references to the house are to be found in such fashion journals such as *La Mode*. In the issue of August 9, 1841, *La Mode* published a fashion plate drawn by Pierre Numa Bassaget, known as Numa, including a woman's riding costume, whose chemise and linen could be had at Doucet (fig. 2.3).

At this point the business was an unabashedly single-family affair, styled Maison Doucet, with members of the family operating departments. Father and sons, as Doucet et fils, conducted a business for the masculine lingerie items, while Mme Doucet (née Adèle Girard, who married Antoine Doucet about 1816) oversaw aspects of accessories for women, including the longstanding lace trade. Fig. 2.3 may be an early reference to the merchandise of Mme Doucet. The skillful products of Antoine and Adèle's combined energies—essentially the embroidered shirts—were of sufficient quality to be awarded a second-class medal at the 1851 Crystal Palace exhibition in London.

The second of Antoine and Adèle Doucet's six offspring, Edouard (1822–98), was to become Jacques Doucet's father and directly carry on the family apparel business. Two of the others were associated with the trade: Clémence, who would marry into a garment-making family, and Albert, who had tailoring shops in 1865 with Van Roey at 13 rue de Bac and 37 rue de Lille, and would later found a competitive branch dealing in linen accessories for men.[6]

In many ways the Doucets were a typical middle-class family, the sons and grandsons becoming tradesmen or military adventurers; competition in the world and family ties, rather than intellectual pursuits, were very likely encouraged. It was probably Albert's son who as "Doucet jeune" conducted the successful men's shirtmaking and other personal-linen concerns from about 1874 on. Men's shirts and accessories bearing the Doucet name appear to be from this business, located at 10 rue Halévy (see p. 167). Recognition came swiftly: a first place at the 1875 international exposition in Santiago, Chile, was followed by a bronze medal at the 1878 Paris Exposition Universelle. International outlets were set up in Alexandria, Buenos Aires, and Santiago. In 1893, the time of another world's fair, a shop was to be found in the host city, Chicago, as well as branches in New York and London. The business was bought in 1896 by a M. Gaudin.

Confirming the evidence on the billhead and prospectus since 1845, a Mme Doucet was listed in the business directories, also operating at 17 rue de la Paix. Her business is likewise identified as selling lingerie for clients of unspecified gender and age. Because no first initial is given, it is a matter of speculation as to whether Adèle was the only female family member in the trade; whether there were two direct lineage generations at work (Adèle and/or Clémence); or whether a daughter-in-law inspired the title. The courtesy title of feminine gender was associated with the address up into the twentieth century—long after Adèle died in 1866, just months before Antoine. Jacques Doucet's own mother, Mathilde, was still alive in 1902.

The 1850s were a time of change on the rue de la Paix. With the renumbering of the street at the beginning of the decade, the new Doucet address became 21. At about the same time, the names of the succeeding generation started to become associated with Antoine's firm. The second son, Edouard, took over as principal of Maison Doucet and briefly merged the firm in 1853[7] with that of Auguste Duclerc, the husband of his only sister, Clémence. For some yet unexplained reason, Duclerc left the operation to Edouard Doucet in 1857. During the four-year partnership, there had been another associate, the tailor Joseph Leblanc.[8] It is clear that Edouard was anxious to reorganize the house according to what might be considered more advanced marketing methods. The house would specialize more and more in men's wear, claiming to be tailors and adding to their list of merchandise cravates, "irrétrécissables" (unshrinkable linens), and handkerchiefs. Then in 1857–58, almost as if sensing the newly established competition of Worth and Bobergh just down the street at number 7, Edouard Doucet appeared in the directory for the first time under "nouveautés confectionnées" for ladies offering "trousseaux, layettes, et manteaux pour dames." "Manteaux" was the all-encompassing word covering fitted, semifitted, and unfitted items of apparel worn as outer attire.

Royal patronage first came to Maison Doucet in the 1850s, not from Empress Eugénie, but from Emperor Napoleon III, who favored Doucet shirts. On invoices for the house, other royal clients are listed in 1857: His Majesty the King of Bavaria, His Majesty the King of the Netherlands, His Imperial Highness the Grand Duke Constantin of Russia.[9]

Edouard was not the only Doucet making men's shirts or other accoutrements at this time. Edouard's brother Albert, mentioned earlier, probably began his career between 1844 and 1847, working from 17 rue de la Paix, where he specialized in plain and embroidered handkerchiefs and foulards (neckerchiefs). His business endeavors appear to have encountered uneven periods but he plodded along, and as has also been mentioned, his son built up perhaps the best-known men's shirtmaking establishment of late nineteenth-century Paris. The following list from the trade directories will give some impression of the number of Doucets participating in the Parisian apparel trade during the second half of the nineteenth century. In 1844–45, a C. Doucet, formerly in association with Duché Aîné et Cie, worked at 28 Notre-Dame de Victoires. For the year 1865, Doucet et Cie, tailors, operated from 49 rue Vivienne and an F. Doucet had shops at 168 rue Saint-Martin and at 23 avenue Daumesnil, where he handled both ready-made and special-order linens for women and children.[10] F. Doucet's business was bought by an

Stamped gold on white petersham, Doucet and Carré impressions
c. 1880s

2.4 Fashion illustration published in 1892 generically inspired by the lingerie section of Maison Doucet. Source unidentified.

Woven pink on white, yellow on black
c. 1890s

E. Gaultier in 1889 and apparently ceased shortly thereafter. Beginning in 1858, a Mme Doucet sold ready-made fashions from 12 rue Mont Thabor, moving between 1870 and 1881 to 28 Notre-Dame de Lorette, where she specialized in "nouveautés confectionnées pour dames" (ready-made fancy articles for women). The last two years of her business were conducted from 6 faubourg Saint-Honoré. Another Doucet business conducted by a woman appears only in the directory for 1865, at 10 rue Lamartine, where one-of-a-kind items for women were made. This address disappeared as a Doucet business for more than a quarter of a century, to reappear in 1891 as a Doucet perfumery. In 1877 only, the name Doucet was attached to the business operating at 88 rue Oberkampf, where chemises and other handmade articles could be acquired. By 1898 an F. Doucet was at 52 rue Oberkampf, merchandising lingerie and shirts for women and children. For the last quarter of the nineteenth century Alfred Doucet, possibly Edouard's brother and Jacques's uncle, worked as a tailor in partnership with Tanneaux at 24 rue Richelieu. Corsets were fitted between 1883 and 1886 by Mme Doucet who occupied 40 rue Francs-Bourgeois; between 1889 and at least 1905, another Mme Doucet was selling custom-made dresses and outerwear at 40 rue Ecuries-d'Artois, while yet another was competitively engaged in dressmaking at 36 rue Beaupaire from at least 1890 on. It should be remembered that listings in the Parisian trade directory were paid for and therefore may not even reflect all the various Doucets in clothing-associated trades during the nineteenth century. Yet some notion of the impact of the name Doucet in the clothing industry may be gleaned from the 1895 directory, which includes thirty commercial entries for Doucet, six of which relate to attiring the public.

In 1858 the Doucet firm, guided by young Edouard, was advertised in the directory under the category "nouveautés confectionnées" as handling trousseaux, layettes, and outer wraps for women. At the same time it was publicly recognized as a longstanding and important Parisian commercial endeavor in the line of men's accessories. A decade later, with the founding father gone, Edouard disposed of the men's haberdashery business; in 1869 Jules L'Hoest and Pilzer acquired the Doucet name and took over the firm, which later became Pilzer et Harson. In this move Edouard gave up the business founded by his late father to concentrate on the related one established by his recently deceased mother. Following in her path, he would at first specialize in lingerie items for women (fig. 2.5, pl. 25).

One of the other occupants of 21 rue de la Paix, from at least 1883, was a Mme Carré, advertising as a couturier, whose business imprint on petershams is frequently found appended to that of Mme Doucet—a rare instance in which two house imprints appear as a single label (see p. 141). Her affiliation with Maison Doucet is unknown, though the name of Carré, like that of Doucet, has a lengthy and tangled linkage with the clothing industry. The most plausible candidate for connection with the Doucets is the Mme Carré who first appears in the 1869 Didot-Bottin operating as Carré et Cie of 16 rue Louis-le-Grand and selling ready-made lingerie, to change later, in 1876, to dresses as well as lingerie, and who appears in the 1878 directory as a couturier operating from the Doucet address on the rue de la Paix.

Throughout the 1860s the name Mme Doucet was associated with both ready-made and special-order lingerie for women. In 1870, just at the end of the Second Empire, the venture, now securely in the hands of Edouard, was credited with creating couture garments, some of sufficient quality to ensnare patronage by the queen of Wurtemberg, and with providing ready-made lingerie to the fashionably aware Empress Eugénie. Such royal patronage may have prompted the proclamation that henceforth Doucet would be creating attire for women of the highest levels of society.

2.5   Maison Doucet day dress in floral-printed lilac foulard, possibly designed by Jacques Doucet, as published in *The Queen* and *L'Art et la Mode* in 1884. Sketch by Marie de Solar.

2.6 Quarterly account rendered to Mrs. John Wanamaker in 1899 by Maison Doucet and noting the passing of Edouard Doucet. The Brooklyn Museum Archives.

Madame

Nous avons l'honneur de vous adresser ci-inclus, pour la bonne règle de nos écritures, notre facture semestrielle de F$_{rs}$ 6580—

que nous recommandons à votre bienveillant accueil.

Nous serons très-heureux que vous nous favorisiez de nouvelles commandes, auxquelles nous réservons nos meilleurs soins.

Nous vous prions d'agréer, Madame, l'expression de nos civilités empressées.

This old account belonging to the Estate of our late sir Ed Doucet, we permit us to insist for a next kind settlement.

J. Doucet.

Stamped gold on black petersham
c. 1890s

It is thought that Jacques Doucet, like his contemporaries the Worth sons, was similarly participating in the family business by the time he reached his majority in 1874 (fig. 2.6). By 1886 Edouard had become a principal in the company, and by 1898, the year in which Edouard died, the Doucet name seems to be the only one associated with the smart address on the ever more fashionable rue de la Paix.

❧◦❧◦❧◦❧◦❧

THE HOUSE

During World War I the House of Doucet was described as maintaining a character of sober and gracious elegance and a fineness of workmanship that could not be surpassed.[1] These attributes closely matched the owner's highly burnished persona, which Jacques Doucet, one of the great art connoisseurs and collectors of his day, had modeled on the modes and manners of the eighteenth century. Laces and fripperies bespeaking the flirtations and seductions associated with that century of romance would become house hallmarks. Unlike its competitors Worth and Pingat, Maison Doucet directed its style toward less structured fabrics, if not garments. Doucet earned recognition for toilettes of accomplished style, constructed with delicate, filmy fabrics, in which contemporary stars of the stage seduced their audiences. While Jacques Doucet is best known for his delicate, feminine toilettes, he has also been credited with creating one of the enduring staples of a woman's wardrobe both in this century and particularly in the last two decades of the previous one: the tailored suit, or *tailleur* (fig. 2.7). The other innovation accorded to Doucet is that of working with furs as if they were fabric, making fitted coats with fur on the outside.[2]

By 1895 the name of Doucet was sufficiently revered that American merchants were buying his models, along with Worth's, to export and copy.

Stamped gold on white petersham
c. 1890–1910

2.7   Maison Doucet suit for travel of drab cotton drill, probably designed by Jacques Doucet, c. 1894. Victoria and Albert Museum. T.15&a–1979.

2.8 Wedding dress worn by Consuelo Vanderbilt on her marriage in 1895 to the duke of Marlborough. The dress was copied from a Doucet model by Mrs. Donovan, a prominent New York City dressmaker. Sketch published in *Harper's Bazar*, Nov. 9, 1895.

"Among the prettiest of these dresses, one imported by Arnold, Constable & Co. has the flowered silk coatwaist gay enough for the calling dress of the bride, or for evening wear at home or at the theatre . . ."[3] Doucet modes to entice were at McCreery's new store in New York, one skirt having a hemline six yards wide.[4] As fate would have it, the garment produced by Maison Doucet that received the most press was a wedding dress it only designed (fig. 2.8). The actual gown was a copy made in 1895 by New York City's most prominent, and socially acceptable, dressmaker and importer, Mrs. Donovan. The eighteen-year-old bride, Consuelo Vanderbilt, came away from the altar as the ninth duchess of Marlborough. Her gown, it was noted, was more elaborate than usual for one of her tender age. Of ivory white satin, it bore several Doucet marks—a full, widely belted waist and an abundance of lace. The garniture of lace had been made on commission in Belgium and was said to pay homage to the land of her husband in its construction technique— point d'Angleterre—and to her maternal ancestors, inasmuch as it copied the subject of their bridal laces.[5]

Of the handful of notable couturiers, a few of the larger ones had a yearly turnover in business of more than thirty million francs. Worth and Doucet were among this select group of those employing more than five hundred pairs of hands in an industry that by 1902 included some two thousand ateliers for made-to-measure creations. With the relatively few remaining garments, it is impossible to deduce what the annual configuration of production was at any given time, although Maison Doucet, in keeping with the practices of other similar concerns, kept track of orders and models through a numbering system. As the century turned, Doucet could claim, as did others of grand couturier status, a branch boutique outside of Paris, on the rue de Paris in the smart resort of Trouville, which catered to members of the courts of Russia, Great Britain, Portugal, Spain, Italy, Austria and Romania.

There is evidence that while Doucet demanded strict practices in his art dealings, more relaxed conditions prevailed at the house. Prices, always exorbitant, were on a very loose sliding scale. Americans carried the greater expenses, although Elisabeth de Gramont, wife of the duc de Clermont-Tonnerre, was encouraged by her husband to pawn her jewels so that she could pay Doucet's bills.[6]

Unlike Worth, Doucet did not participate in the memorable Paris Exposition Universelle of 1900. The two houses would have a link, however, in the person of Paul Poiret, who was employed at Doucet from 1896 until 1900, when the young designer joined Maison Worth. Doucet's influence was the greater in shaping the future of Poiret, who mimicked his employer's appearance—adopting Doucet's beard and mirror-polished leather shoes, and going so far as to put himself in the hands of the same tailor. Poiret had sold some sketches to the house before being hired; his designs fitted in perfectly with the decor and style of Maison Doucet. In its Rococo salons draped with pink muslin curtains—which had been redecorated in 1880, according to *Vogue* in 1915—the cocottes of the day would be smothered in laces, ribbons, spangles, tulle, and silk organza in soft pastel shades. The strong wills of the two designers, senior and junior, would cause a parting of the ways in 1900, but only after Poiret had absorbed many of the administrative details attendant to the management of a house of haute couture. Interestingly, neither of their establishments would productively survive World War I, but for different reasons. While Poiret's ego and extravagances lay behind his house's decline, Doucet's fashions did not keep up with the times. Doucet had had the luck to land in a dress-designing era that initially melded with his own artistic sensibilities—one in which the richly elegant days of the previous century were taken as a measure for greatness in all aspects of culture. And the house's longstanding association with fluid fabrics made Maison Doucet a natural for designing the supple,

2.9 At-home "Empire" dress for a young woman, 1892. Source unidentified.

Woven gold on white, silvery gray on white, white on black tape
c. 1900 on

sensuous gowns of the Art Nouveau aesthetic. But while Jacques Doucet as a collector would step boldly into the avant-garde in the second decade of the twentieth century, with his astute eye for the sleek angularity of abstract art, he, remarkably, never was able to see the possibilities for translating the same lines into clothing design. For him women should be cloaked in undulating lines and fabrics with traditional feminine associations: laces, ribbons, chiffons, and organza (pls. 30, 31). Not for Doucet was the rising skirt or the angular, simple lines that had been initiated by his protégé Poiret prior to World War I and would come out of the War more firmly ingrained.

Standing in Jacques Doucet's shadow at the house throughout the 1870s to the 1920s was M. José de la Peña de Guzman (Pepe or Pepito, to longstanding friends), the house fitter and a designer, in whose little fingers Poiret saw flashes of brilliance unmatched by Maison Doucet's titular leader. Most of the house fittings were executed by de la Peña in a ritualistic "dance" lasting anywhere from minutes to several hours. It was he who quelled a staff strike in 1901, when the disruption reached such proportions that the house needed to be guarded by the Parisian *gendarmes*.

By having Maison Doucet in the capable hands of de la Peña and Charles Pardinel, who oversaw the house's administrative responsibilities, Jacques Doucet was able to participate as an absentee creative and administrative director. But benign neglect, along with the failure to keep in step with the postwar generation of freer-spirited females who rejected the encumbrance of frills and flounces, led to the inevitable termination of the house. When the establishment was merged with a lesser house, Doueillet, in 1924, it was predictable that the name Doucet would soon completely vanish from the ranks of haute couture. The combined house ceased operation in 1932. If a successor to the House of Doucet is to be proposed, the honor must go to Jacques's other brilliant assistant, the inventive Madeleine Vionnet, who was hired in 1907. Her very first collection with Doucet is said to have been revolutionary, as the staid house presented thinly veiled, barefooted mannequins who sashayed before clients in the coming mode of uncorseted figures. Vionnet was to set up her own successful and long-lived house in 1912. Her perfection of fluid, bias-cut garments, frequently executed in filmy fabrics and pale tints, hark back to her training with Doucet.

JACQUES DOUCET

Jacques Doucet (fig. 2.10) was a man of strong passions: a drive for self-perfection; an aversion to the association of being in trade; and an appetite for the hunt and capture of art objects. What conspired to impel Doucet in these directions is an unknown as what went on during the first half of his life.

In a rather ambiguous comment, Jacques Doucet stated that he grew up among pigs.[1] It is not clear whether he meant, factually, that his childhood was spent in the countryside or that he found his family life in Paris so physically and intellectually unsympathetic as to evoke the image of a sty. It might be said that home was one and the same as Maison Doucet. Jacques had literally been born in the business; the birth occurred February 19, 1853, at the Maison Doucet premises of 21 rue de la Paix. Edouard Doucet and Mathilde Gonnard had been married just a year before the arrival of their first, and surviving, son. There was to be a daughter Marie, born in 1854, and a younger son, Maurice, born in 1861, who died in infancy.

The one known boyhood interest of Jacques was painting, an avenue of expression shared by Jean-Phillipe Worth. Growing up at 7 rue de la Paix, the Worth boys were just doors away from young Doucet, at number 21. The offspring of the two families must have been exposed to remarkably similar upbringings, and the youths may well have shared activities and adventures (although there is little evidence of interaction in later life). As sons and heirs, both the Worth boys and Jacques Doucet appear to have been expected to participate in their respective family operations on completion of secondary school. While the Worths accepted the yoke of business and pulled it along in a straight and unswerving path, for Doucet the obligation was onerous. Where the Worths were satisfied with fleeting forays into the past, Doucet sought personal immersion. Where the Worths could hardly keep up with the present, Doucet leapt into the future, at least in his pursuits as an art connoisseur and collector. The Worths were committed to the art of dressmaking, Jacques Doucet to art.

Apparently Jacques Doucet could only be called an aspiring painter, and as offensive as he seems to have found the family enterprise, it at least offered him an outlet for creativity and, perhaps more important, the income to pursue the visual arts from another direction. With money he could buy his way into the art world, although money would not buy what was innate to Jacques Doucet: an unerring eye. Almost with his nose buried in books and his mind and heart deeply distracted by art of the past and then the future, Jacques Doucet successfully guided the couture establishment of Maison Doucet to the top of the profession.

2.10   Jacques Doucet, one of seven "Great Dressmakers of Paris," pictured in an engraving in the *New York Herald*, April 5, 1896.

149

2.11 An open robe of the Louis XV period from the Jacques Doucet Collection. Sketched by Maurice Leloir on presentation to La Société de l'Histoire du Costume in 1907–9.

For years the arts and decoration of his native France in the eighteenth century fascinated Doucet, and he extended his collecting and business interests to encompass even garments from this epoch. As one of the Société de l'Histoire du Costume's founders, officials, and donors, Doucet is closely associated with the garments of the Louis of the eighteenth century. Between 1907 and 1909 he donated to this organization what were described as a white satin gown and one of red broché silk, both of the Louis XV period, and a broché silk skirt of the Louis XVI epoch (fig. 2.11).[2]

Doucet's avid acquisition of eighteenth-century artifacts appears to have begun about 1896, and for over a decade he worked to build one of the most staggeringly beautiful collections of this material; ultimately this collection would be ranked alongside the Wallace Collection in London. The question may be asked if Doucet became interested in the art he eventually collected through the applied art of dress design. Many of the items fabricated by Maison Doucet were based on historical prototypes, and indeed, at the very moment young Doucet became involved in the house, feminine fashions were being inspired by images of seventeenth- and eighteenth-century derivation.

Living among his treasures, Doucet at first resided in a small house at 27 rue de la Ville l'Evêque. A grand house was specially constructed in 1906 at 19 rue Spontini to display the works of the Louis XV and XVI epoch: pictures and drawings by Watteau, Boucher, Fantin-Latour, and Fragonard; genre pictures and landscapes by Chardin; furniture by such eighteenth-century *ébénistes* of the first order as Reisener, Leleu, and Charlin. Accounts have it that circumstances connected with an inamorata somehow precipitated one of the most remarkable art sales of this century in 1912, when Doucet sold most of his collection.[3] After a brief flirtation with the works of the French Impressionists, Doucet then made a bold and brave foray into the unchartered field of contemporary art. Fascinated by the works of Degas, Cézanne, Monet, Matisse, van Gogh, Picasso, Braque, Derain, de Chirico, Miró, Ernst, Picabia, and others, he brought to his collection such landmarks of twentieth-century painting as Picasso's *Demoiselles d'Avignon* and Rousseau's *La Joueuse de Flute*. These works of art were displayed from 1913 on, in the apartment he occupied at 46 avenue du Bois and, later, also in the studio he acquired on grounds in Neuilly. These studio quarters were turned into galleries decorated by Pierre Legrain and Rose Adler. Also displayed, as in some Renaissance cabinet of curiosities, were such disparate objects as African tribal artifacts, Lalique glass, Persian ceramics, and archaic Chinese paintings. Doucet welcomed fellow enthusiasts to view his holdings, enjoying the exchange but possibly reveling more in the awe his collections raised. The American collector and artist Aline Meyer Liebman recorded in her diary impressions of her visits to Doucet just before he died in 1929: "At Jacques Doucet's house, saw entrance hall—floor of silvered material glass-covered put in rectangular forms—with inlay of red glass or other material—perfectly stunning. Staircase the most beautiful thing I have seen.—Steel or aluminum in wonderful design with panels of black engraved glass.—Clock by Legrain with top of beautifully arranged glass strips in lovely color effects lighted from behind. Door made of cylindrical glass tubing backed with plate glass.—Designed by Legrain & Doucet."[4]

By the time Doucet was recognized as a serious and important collector and salon leader, the family business and real estate investment had given

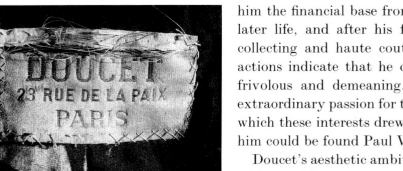

Woven gold on white
c. 1910

him the financial base from which to build his art empire. Throughout his later life, and after his father's death, Jacques attempted to keep his collecting and haute couture interests thoroughly separate. Subsequent actions indicate that he came to regard any association with fashion as frivolous and demeaning. Few of his dressmaking clients knew of his extraordinary passion for the visual and decorative arts[5] and the circles into which these interests drew him. In the literary coterie that formed around him could be found Paul Valéry, Pierre Loüys, and Henri de Régnier.

Doucet's aesthetic ambitions were reflected in his appearance. He dressed with exquisite taste, too precious for many but certainly in keeping with his aesthete persona. He would appear in white spats, white waistcoat, and a beard so perfectly clipped that it was likened to the trimmings of a royal park (fig. 2.12). From head to toe he was perfectly turned out: his shoes were relacquered daily and left to dry in the oven. Elisabeth de Gramont recalled the highly polished footwear: to her M. Jacques—the familiar name many clients and colleagues used—was a charming man, very well dressed, elegant, affable, and with impeccable manners, but his shoes were just a bit too well varnished.[6]

Most found Doucet the man almost totally removed from his couture business. He could be quite generous, nevertheless; his advance of Fr 500 to Paul Poiret aroused such suspicion that the young designer's father personally went back to check on the source. Staff found that he was demanding, a perfectionist who sought the exquisite and the refined. He always thought of himself as a discerning collector, never as a simple dressmaker or even a *grand couturier*. As the actress and client Réjane remarked, "Today he is the Prince of Wales . . . or the King of England."[7] Hiding his true identity, Doucet listed himself in the Paris telephone directory of 1895 as retired.

In 1923, at age seventy, Doucet was offered the Légion d'honneur, an accolade he refused. Only four years before he had married Jeanne Roger, a woman who shared his collecting instincts even if she was not the love of his life. In August 1928, he removed to Mme Doucet's home at 33 rue Saint-James, Neuilly. There he indulged in one final rush of collecting and decorating before his death on October 30, 1929.

❧◦❧◦❧◦❧◦❧

DESIGNS

Information about designs from Jacques Doucet's early years at Maison Doucet is sparse. It is impossible to pinpoint the moment when Jacques Doucet assumed either primary or secondary management or design responsibilities within his family's diversified establishment. Like the Worth sons, Jacques would seem to have been formally initiated into the activities of the house shortly after the fall of the Second Empire, but even as late as 1894, fashion correspondents do not give readers a clue as to whether dealings are with the elder or younger Doucet, so secure are they that their readers are versed in the knowledge of exactly who is "Doucet, the famous dressmaker."

153

Furthermore, while family members of the firm are documented as having created custom garments since at least 1870, it is not until the 1880s that either visual evidence or extant garments confirm this activity.

Those dresses that have survived carry, in keeping with the higher-quality dressmaking tradition of the time, a label identifying the house at the internal waistline: for Doucet, a slightly old-fashioned stamped petersham label with gold lettering on white silk (see p. 145). This label would remain a house trademark well up into the twentieth century. Wraps of the same era carry woven ribbon labels inscribed with the house name and address (see p. 142). The stamped labels with the Mme Doucet configuration sometimes additionally inform us the house is patronized by many of the world's courts (see p. 137). As has been noted, these Mme Doucet labels are frequently abutted by a similar stamp with the impression of Mme Carré (see p. 141).

2.13 (*Above*) Maison Doucet day dress in dark green cashmere, possibly designed by Jacques Doucet, published in *L'Art et la mode* in 1884. Sketch by Marie de Solar.

2.14 (*Right*) Maison Doucet evening dress in pekin moiré, probably designed by Jacques Doucet and inspired by a 1780s gown, 1892. Source unidentified.

The earliest images of Doucet garments from the time of Jacques yet located are to be found in the lively sketches of fashions drawn for 1884 issues of *L'Art et la mode* (fig. 2.13). An illustrated toilette for early summer is described as "lilac foulard, studded with a small white flower. The underskirt is bordered with a kilting and bouillonné; the deep tunic is accordion [pleated], kilted from the waist, and edged with lace. It is draped so as to form a fan-shaped tablier; bodice with full bib outlined with velvet, and laced with silk cord." The July 19, 1884, issue of *The Queen* carries, alongside the repeated sketch, an advertisement for two patterns—bodice for two shillings, seven pence, skirt and tunic for three shillings, one penny—which, when made up, would give the dressmaker this very style. A second illustrated Doucet dress from 1884—a daytime gown—is described as of grand simplicity and great elegance, fabricated from dark green cashmere. A latticework of interwoven cloth and gilt galloon is used as a banding at the hemline and as a stomacher.

The largest selection of Doucet garments from the 1880s seems to be in the collections of the Cincinnati Art Museum. With the exception of a heavy, sober, cut-velvet dolman mantle at the Musée de la Mode et du Costume, Paris (65.86.1), the extant articles of attire from this decade are in accord with the light, fluffed and flounced lingerie for which the house had been known. Machine-made laces frill and flow over the confections of supple fabrics in creamy white and pastels that sweep and swag around the body from neck to toe. Sketches indicate that Doucet's 1880s garments, when not so conceived, were notably severe day dresses that were devoid of the heavy, dense applied surface decoration and/or layering of fabric(s) associated with this epoch. The more formal garments were meant to meld into the equally excessive interior decorations of the period: remarkably, dress and decor assisted each other in presenting a harmonious whole.

At the beginning of the 1890s, editorial and engraved pictorial citations on Doucet multiply (fig. 2.14); the former remain the more common references until the turn of the century, when photographs appear. Generally the mannequins for these camera images were French actresses—many established house associates—whose portraits in Doucet toilettes graced either theatrical or fashion reviews.

Models imported in 1892 (fig. 2.15) for Americans, always important Doucet clients, included a "charmingly simple dress . . . of Russian red vigogne with a round waist, large sleeves, and bell skirt, trimmed with jet galloon and the gay Bulgarian embroidery seen on écru linen towels," or the dress of bright red crepon meant only for the house; they could be selected at a New York dress emporium.[1] The Costume Institute of Kyoto, Japan, possesses a vibrant red day dress with self-colored moiré-ribbon stripes (80.23.1), which, except for a sizable bow at the throat and a row of minor

2.15 Maison Doucet winter walking suit in wool cloth with caracul trim, probably designed by Jacques Doucet and inspired by a man's late eighteenth-century greatcoat, 1892. Source unidentified.

2.16 Copy of a Jacques Doucet promenade dress in changeable mauve taffeta, inspired by an 1830s gown. Sketched by Mathilde Sey for the *Paris Herald*, c. 1895.

ones at the hem, fits in with the coloration, but is uncharacteristic of the house, of garments from the 1892 models. Among the New York City shops importing Doucets to use as models were Mrs. Donovan and Mme Barnes, and carriage-trade stores like Lord & Taylor and Arnold, Constable & Co.

As one might expect, Doucet was one of the first of the great French couturiers to utilize supple silks, which would spiral around the figure, giving the impression of an unfurling hollyhock bloom. Especially suitable was a satin long associated with the well-known London firm of Liberty & Co. For decades, when international fashions were defined by stiffly rigid, woven patterned fabrics, Liberty's had specialized in fluid, effortlessly draping goods. Not only was the hand of the material in keeping with the taste of Maison Doucet, but the colorways also matched house predilections. One

156

fabric that Doucet did not do well by, judging from comment, was a summer-weight crepon; Paquin and Doucet used very little in the summer of 1895, "and there is no reason to suppose they will take any more kindly to that unsatisfactory material for the coming· season. It doesn't wear well, it is neither dress nor undress, it is far from effective."[2] In the fall of 1895 Doucet was, according to the Paris correspondent for *Harper's Bazar*, "showing ·marvelous *déshabillés* of embroidered crapes, made with Watteau pleats down the back, tight-fitting sides, and entirely loose fronts, with high Medicis collar bordered with fur."[3] The fall season brought eighteenth-century adaptations, at least at Doucet (one fashion observer found that at three of the leading houses—Beer, Doucet, and Paquin—the styles were as absolutely different as though they had been created in different parts of the world, in different years): "For those who prefer a single color—and for black dresses so becoming to young and middle-aged alike, Doucet combines different materials—satin, brocade & velvet, all of one color—in one gown (fig. 2.16). Thus a black velvet Louis XVI with short circular basque, flaring collar, puff of white tulle, and white satin. Sleeves have butterfly puffs of velvet. Skirt of new moiré with dull satin ground, the watering forming a quaint design of large stiff detached flowers. Ecru net for plastron."[4] Such fashions—made known by dressmakers who, like New York's Mme Barnes, had visited the Parisian workshops of Paquin, Doucet, Raudnitz, Beer, and others—were described in *Harper's Bazar*: "The new gowns are composition in style. They represent the dress worn under . . . Louis XIV, Louis XV, and Louis XVI of France (fig. 2.17). Some gowns have features taken from the styles of each of these three reigns but there are Louis XVI dresses imported that are literal copies of those worn by Marie Antoinette and the beautiful women of her court. Other dresses similarly will, however, omit the striking feature of the originals and will have large-topped sleeves not unlike those of recent seasons."[5] Revivals always carry a bit of their own time: while large leg-of-mutton sleeves would have seemed preposterous to the unlucky queen, such transgressions were seen in 1895 as exceedingly chic and simply constructed, and were recommended for dignified women of middle age. It seems there was some hesitancy in 1895 as to the stance the house would take over the grossly enlarged sleeve caps of the day. In January they were promoting a "mutton leg" sleeve, which in an imported model—suitable for afternoon or informal dinner wear—could be taken south as a model for spring dresses late in the year.[6] By June the same customers are encouraged to try a gown "somewhat in the Marie Antoinette fashion, but the sleeves are extra large gigot, gathered the entire length of the arm to 'mousquetaire' them—as a sales woman says to wrinkle them around the arm."[7] The outrageously enlarged sleeves of the mid-nineties would deflate, and only weeks later, Doucet followers were advised, "Sleeves have already become less in *l'air*, and

2.17 Jacques Doucet. *Evening Dress*, c. 1902. Pink silk damask patterned with bowed foliate sprays; machine-made lace and velvet trim. Inspired by a mid-eighteenth-century open robe. Worn by Caroline Schermerhorn Astor Wilson. The Metropolitan Museum of Art, Gift of Orme and R. Thornton Wilson in memory of their mother, Caroline Schermerhorn Astor Wilson, 49.3.26.

Doucet has been making them lately very drooping indeed and making his coats entirely without godets in the back."⁸

Over the last few years of the nineteenth century, many of the editorial citations are for blouses only. In one instance the house distinguished itself by using two yards of four-inch-wide lace to drape pointed frills over the outside of a neckband.⁹

From the end of the century is a salmon velvet evening frock that belonged to Caroline Schermerhorn Astor Wilson (fig. 2.18). Rambling over the gown are rambunctiously wild tiger lilies, held in place by an equally exuberant undulating border. The blooms are embroidered with green and purple silks and set with silvered sequins. Fairly dripping from the neckline is a bertha of lace and chiffon. While it now does not carry a Doucet label, an evening cape in the Museum of London (fig. 2.19) has traditional and design associations with the house and is kindred to the Schermerhorn gown. Folded along the shoulder-arm line, the cape resembles an inverted fan in both shape and construction. The neckline—analogous to the rivet and gorge of a fan—has an outline of white ostrich feathers on a high-standing appliquéd flaring collar. Comparable to the area of the fan's sticks is a delicately hand-painted

2.18 (*Opposite*) Jacques Doucet. *Evening Toilette*, c. 1899. Salmon pink silk velvet embroidered in Art Nouveau tiger-lily motif; silk chiffon, bobbin-tape lace. Worn by Caroline Schermerhorn Astor Wilson. The Metropolitan Museum of Art, Gift of Orme and R. Thornton Wilson in memory of their mother, Caroline Schermerhorn Astor Wilson, 49.3.27 .

2.19 Attributed to Jacques Doucet. *Opera Cape*, c. 1899. Silk, painted with Art Nouveau floral motifs; appliqués, silk georgette and machine-made Chantilly lace. Museum of London, Museum Purchase, 86.19/1.

Stamped gold on white cotton tape, for lingerie dresses

cream silk taffeta with representations of stylized billowing blossoms, probably peonies. This artwork is initialed *F.C.* Immediately below, resembling the fan's shoulder, is a band of black appliquéd floral lace cutouts sparkling with beads of jet and cut steel. For the leaf area, found here at the hipline, there are flounced, pouffed, and scalloped rows of deep orchid velvet, white ostrich, black Chantilly lace laid over pleated white gauze and cream satin. Perhaps, from the vantage point of today's stripped-down and angular aesthetics, this cape represents the excesses espoused in the late nineteenth century, but in its own time it was undoubtedly revered as the epitome of the dressmaker's art.

For the curvilinear motifs so much a part of the Art Nouveau aesthetic that affected Doucet's fin de siècle designs, nature provided a ready-made bounty of resources. With its twining tendrils, the grape was an ideal subject, and Doucet applied representations of clusters of the fruit to garments for all occasions. Within his subdued, refined palette, which frequently was related to the golds and silvers of precious metals, he would put forth either matte or brilliant examples of these colors. In one evening gown uniting an applied grape motif in full-blown, domed paillettes of silver on a silvery net and silk chiffon ground, he left the grapes as if clambering along a trellis open to the sky (The Metropolitan Museum of Art, 44.64.56). Machine-worked eyelet embroidery gives a negative impression of grape clusters as they border the edges of an afternoon ensemble, whose body is midnight blue stamped velvet impressed in a large-scale vermiculate motif (pl. 32). The height of the silversmith's art at the turn of the century is manifest in metal-shot dresses. Under candle-, gas-, or the relatively new electric light, Mrs. Perry Belmont must have appeared as a statuette dipped in gold in her closely fitted gown, whose surface was relieved but enriched by cream silk-twist embroidery of peonies worked in a manner not dissimilar to that on Chinese-ornamented "Spanish" shawls (pl. 26). The second gown is of silver cloth now distorted by the textile's manufacturing techniques but, happily, still conveying some of the original sheen (The Brooklyn Museum, 65.184.63). Almost as if taking inspiration from the turquoise-and-silver jewelry of American Indians of the southwest, Doucet has applied to the fabric chunky opaque beads of aqua glass, but in a European floral design arrangement.

In house designs of the period, surface decoration is as important as the pliability of the fabrics and appliqués are prominent. Aside from the passementerie often used, toilettes display three-dimensional flowers formed from ribbons (pl. 27), rosettes of chiffon and China silk, and even a realistic swarm of bees buzzing their way up from the dipping hemline of an evening dress from about 1900 (fig. 2.20).

It is frequently difficult to distinguish the fabric of a tablecloth or glass curtain from that of the turn-of-the-century garment known as the lingerie

2.20 Jacques Doucet. *Evening Toilette*, c. 1900. White mousseline de soie embroidered with bee motifs; machine-made lace. Union Française des Arts du Costume, Gift of De Bray.

dress, which served mothers and daughters for well over a generation as the uniform summertime frock. Some of these dresses were fabricated from snippets of antique and/or modern embroideries and/or laces, which were united within a framework of cotton or linen. Others were composed almost exclusively of the laces currently in vogue: Irish crochet and tape. Doucet's lingerie dresses are banquets for the eye, with the good possibility of indigestion. In one example dated to 1900, a jungle of design elements in needle- and lacework is juxtaposed with an embroidered cratered ground (The Brooklyn Museum, 65.184.9). The background itself is a dotted eyelet on which stylized floral motifs have been worked in embroidery stitches imitating the pattern and technique of Venetian gros point lace, even mimicking applied three-dimensional petals and the needle-lace fillings that are so distinctive of this category of lace. Inserted medallions grapple for space within the meander of a Maltese lace band. For another day dress of this period, the house used cascades of Irish crochet (fig. 2.21). The barely defined stylized floral motif of the lace flows over enlarged puffed, capped sleeves and a considerable expanse of pouter-pigeon monobosom. Momentary surcease comes at the plain, draped, satin-faced ribbon cummerbund. Among dresses of their type, both of these garments represent a pinnacle of overstatement.

In general, the rustle of silks so synonymous with the fin de siècle was more characteristic of the taffetas and satins espoused by Worth and other competitors than of the subtle sheathing of supple silks favored by the house under Jacques Doucet. Of all the Parisian couture establishments in operation at the turn of the century, the House of Doucet perhaps best understood how to translate the fluid lines of Art Nouveau into garments that were as eloquent as the decorative forms of the day.

2.21 Jacques Doucet. *Afternoon Dress*, c. 1905. Two varieties of Irish crochet; machine-made laces, satin-face ribbon. Museum of Fine Arts, Boston, Gift of Nathaniel T. Dexter, 1987. 635.

CLIENTS

For those women of fashion who easily affected melting and swooning, Maison Doucet provided sympathetic attire: soft, sweeping, transparent toilettes easily crushed in a harsh world. Like eighteenth-century porcelain figurines, the women so dressed might give the illusion of fragility, but behind the delicacy of a Doucet outfit might stand a woman of cast-iron determination or an ingenue of unsuspected complexities. Indeed, those who wore Doucet toilettes are as intriguing as the garments themselves.

Perhaps because he inhabited environments as artful as stage sets, Jacques Doucet found special reward in the challenge of dressing the great actresses of his day for their theatrical roles. The name Doucet is as inseparable from French fin de siècle theater as that of Worth is from American heiresses.

Of all the Doucet clients—in front of the footlights or otherwise—there is one whose name is so linked with the house and the man that the complexities of their relationship are obscured. She was Réjane, the great presence of the French comedic theater, second only to Sarah Bernhardt in her capacity to draw audiences (fig. 2.22). Born Gabrielle-Charlotte Réju (1856–1920), she had been introduced to couture garments as a young drama student. Her first such dress, from Laferrière, was a simple but expensive cotton frock in which to audition for the renowned Comédie Française. When she was not taken into that company, she switched to the Théâtre du Vaudeville, where she became a fixture in the light comedies of the day, in which the heroine moved facilely between spouse and lover. Such situations were perfect vehicles for Doucet garments: while Worth dressed nouveaux riches and royals who wished to exude status, and Pingat, intellectually agressive women, Doucet was the dominion of the seductive female. By 1885, as Réjane began her romantic liaison with the actor-manager Porel (Désiré Paul Parfouru, called Porel, whom she married about 1890), she became a client of Maison Doucet, having been introduced to the house by her lover. To Réjane must go no small credit for promoting the creations of Maison Doucet. She remained a staunch supporter of the house for decades, appearing both on and off the stage in airily dainty confections loosely based on eighteenth-century prototypes but with touches of Art Nouveau. Her son and biographer, Jacques Porel (also Doucet's godson and namesake) recalls his mother's refrain, after successful ventures to the house, to the effect that Doucet had made her another masterpiece.[1] For this favored client, Jacques Doucet himself would participate in fittings, often having just disembarked from his two-in-hand, which he drove himself. The pair would huddle for a time in the fitting room while the staff shuffled fabrics and finishings on command. Doucet would arrange the dress while the *essayeuses* (fitters) were on their knees, pins at the ready, with Doucet giving orders to his girls in his uniquely strident nasal voice. *Zaza* (1898) is among the productions for which Doucet dressed Réjane.

2.22 Doucet's premier client, the actress Réjane, being fitted at Maison Doucet. Photographed for *Femina*, Dec. 1, 1903.

In 1906, about the time Réjane founded her own theater, the Théâtre Réjane, her relationship with Doucet cooled. It was not until several years after Doucet's great auction in 1912 that it fully resumed. At the moment of her death in 1920, however, the elegancies of her stage costumes and personal wardrobe were remembered almost as much as her acting, for their harmonizing colors, fantasy, wit, charm, and grace—all characteristics of Doucet confections. The cry went out that the great French couturiers had lost not only a friend but also a most valuable collaborator; in reality, the loss affected only one, Doucet.

Dressing chez Doucet would also prove advantageous for Sarah Bernhardt, although that actress, by her own admission, seems to have only been able to command audiences with Doucet fitters and *premiers*, not the master himself. The house oversaw her costumes for productions of *La Dame aux Camélias* and *Frou-Frou*.

The limelight also frequently shone on Cécile Sorel, as dressed by Doucet. Both she and Réjane appeared in *Madame Sans-Gêne* in creations from the house. Mlle Drunzer, whose stage outfits are illustrated in *La Mode pratique*, was another theatrical luminary who appeared in Doucet creations.

Other notable stage personalities who sought the balm of a Doucet were Cléo de Mérode, Rosa Bruck (in the 1901 production of *Yvette*), Jeanne Thomassin, Emiliene d'Alencon, La Belle Otéro, Marguerite Brésil, Marcelle

Lender, Marthé Regnier, Susanne de Behr, and Suzanne Despres. The names of these cocottes and actresses are linked with Doucet's in theater programs and fashion journals of the day, especially *Les Modes* and *La Nouvelle Mode*, and through the camera eye of great photographers like Paul Nadar. One of Cléo de Mérode's evening gowns, fashioned from a delicately printed white silk chiffon strewn with horseshoe-shaped floral arrangements and topped with a stiff satin bertha embroidered with multicolored ribbon strings in floral sprays, is maintained by the Musée de la Mode et du Costume, Paris (fig. 2.23). Unknown to us is whether this slight gown was a garment for the stage or one from Mlle de Mérode's personal wardrobe.

Surviving theatrical outfits from the house are rare, but several do exist; they were probably commissioned in the teens of this century for some production set in the first French Empire (Musée de la Mode et du Costume, Paris, 86.138.6 and 86.138.8). One of the gowns (86.138.8) was designed for a member of the imperial court.

The actress Liane de Pougy proffered in her reminiscences some harsh and unflattering opinions on her dressmaker and repeated the accurate contemporary gossip that Doucet was not very interested in his couture house, but she does not relate what consumed his passion. Using words that are hard to associate with one of the *grandes cocottes* of her day, she observed, "Doucet fitted us out like good mothers of families—or like colonels' ladies"[2]—hardly the images conveyed to us by the press and the many extant garments in which only the astonishingly voluptuous *femmes fatales* of the Belle Epoque could flaunt their feminity.

Other French clients of the house included the fashion-hungry Princess Mathilde, Princess Murat, Comtesse de Greffulhe, Comtesse de la Ribolisière, Mme Verdé de l'Isle, Mme de la Ville Roulx, Mme Jeanne Blanchenay, Mme Henri Viguier,[3] of the family that managed the Parisian department store Hôtel de Ville, and the mother and daughter Baronne Rochetaille and Duchesse de Broglie. From the aristocracy came other clients like Mlle de Contades, who on her marriage to Arthur de Vogué sought the services of the establishment; Mme Doucet made her trousseau, while Mme Laferrière created the dresses.

Doucet's American clients tend to be anonymous more often than those allied to Worth, and as might be expected, there is an overlap of allegiance. Chicago's Abbie Louise Eddy, who had been dealing with the great Parisian haute couture houses since at least 1878, advised her friend Frances Macbeth Glessner (Mrs. John Jacob Glessner) as she embarked on a European journey in 1890: "*Doucet*, Rue de la Paix for dresses: and the tea gowns the finest in the world they won't keep their word however at this place—but sometimes patience is rewarded beautifully."[4] The extremely cosmopolitan Jessie Robbins, who married first Henry Sloane before a sensational divorce united

Woven brown on white, gun metal gray on white ribbon
c. 1910 on

2.23 (*Opposite*) Jacques Doucet. *Gown*, c. 1905. White mousseline de soie printed with rose garlands; embroidered bertha. Worn by the cocotte-actress Cléo de Mérode. Musée de la Mode et du Costume, Gift of Cléo de Mérode, 61.103.5.

2.24 Jacques Doucet. *Evening Gown*, c. 1900.
Strawberry cream panne silk velvet; silver-sequin-embroidered floral motif, appliquéd net, pink chiffon. Worn by Caroline Schermerhorn Astor Wilson. The Metropolitan Museum of Art, Gift of Orme and R. Thornton Wilson in memory of their mother, Caroline Schermerhorn Astor Wilson, 49.3.30.

her with Perry Belmont, had an extensive and quietly elegant wardrobe from Doucet (pl. 26). Members of the New York City merchandising family that founded the notable carriage-trade dry-goods firm of Arnold, Constable & Co. were fitted by Doucet (pls. 29, 31, 32). One daughter, Marie Louise, of the last Constable tied to the business, Frederick Augustus, wore a sea mist tulle latticed with forget-me-nots, in an ethereal creation from the house (The Metropolitan Museum of Art, 47.25.1). Both her mother and sister were also patrons, and the remains of their wardrobes are distributed between the collections of The Metropolitan Museum of Art and The Brooklyn Museum.

Of all the American names tied to Doucet, two members of the Vanderbilt family appear most frequently: Edith Stuyvesant Vanderbilt Gerry and, of course, Consuelo Vanderbilt. Astors were not to be upstaged: Caroline Schermerhorn Astor Wilson indulged in Doucets before and after her marriage (fig. 2.24). Today some of her Doucet wardrobe is scattered among the Smithsonian Institution, The Metropolitan Museum of Art, and The Brooklyn Museum. The range of the Wilson garments, outstanding among extant examples, gives us the clearest impression of the brilliance achieved by the house at the turn of the century. Caroline's mother was comfortable in the respectable, conventional fabrics and fashions of Worth, but for the daughter, a creature of the Belle Epoque, the undulating, swishing, and sweeping garments of Doucet were far more à la mode.

Even fictional creatures of fashion coveted Doucets, and a major exponent of the wares of the house was the literary and fashion savant, Edith Wharton. Her heroine in *The House of Mirth*, Miss Lily Bart, is accused of being in ill humor, perhaps because her last box of Doucet dresses is a failure. In fact, her depression is caused by having to abstain from indulgence in Doucet's frivolities: "I can't afford it. In fact I can't afford any of the things my friends do, . . . I am not as smartly dressed as the other women."[5]

Wherever the fashionable assembled, from the great houses of New York and London to the equally splendid "cottages" of Newport, from the country houses of the British countryside to the chateaux of France and the great resorts and spas of Europe, the *élégantes* appeared in Doucets. "One of the charms of Royat-les-Bains [in the Auvergne region of France]," reported a fashion correspondent, "is that it is free from self consciousness. . . . The women go down to the waters in fearful and wonderful toilettes, and sit in the stocks for feet douches in the department of hydrotherapy in Doucet frocks and Virot bonnets . . ."[6]

Woven red on white cotton, for men's haberdashery
20th century

◆❧◦❦◆ ◆❧◦❦◆ ◆❧◦❦◆ ◆❧◦❦◆

167

Plate 25   Jacques Doucet(?) for Maison Doucet. *Reception Dress*, c. 1888. Silk faille; silk chiffon, machine-made lace. Cincinnati Art Museum, Gift of Mrs. Chase H. Davis, 1958.37

Plate 26   Jacques Doucet. *Ball Gown*, c. 1900. Cloth of gold embroidered with silk twist; machine-made lace. Worn by Mrs. Perry Belmont. The Brooklyn Museum, Gift of Mrs. Daniel McKeon and Mr. Robert Hoguet, Jr., 65.184.64

Plate 27   Jacques Doucet. *Ball Gown*, c. 1902. Silk organza; appliquéd ribbons, embroidery, and beading. Worn by Mrs. Frederick Prince. The Brooklyn Museum, Gift of Mrs. Frederick Prince, Jr., 67.110.182

Plates 28, 29   Jacques Doucet. *Evening Dress*, c. 1902. Silk velvet and net; appliquéd floral motifs, silk ribbon trim. Worn by Mrs. Frederick Augustus Constable (née Louise Bolmer), whose husband managed Arnold, Constable & Co., a New York City department store that imported Doucets. The Brooklyn Museum, Gift of Mrs. Robert G. Olmsted and Constable MacCracken, 65.239.7

Plates 30, 31   Jacques Doucet. *Afternoon Dress*, c. 1903. Silk chiffon and velvet; machine embroidered net, fringe. Worn by Marie Louise or Edith Constable, daughters of the founder, and subsequently the owners, of Arnold, Constable & Co. The Brooklyn Museum, Gift of Mrs. Robert G. Olmsted and Constable MacCracken, 65.239.12

Plate 32   Jacques Doucet. *Visting Dress*, c. 1902. Silk stamped velvet in vermiculate pattern; taffeta eyelet, machine-made lace. Worn by Mrs. Frederick Augustus Constable. The Brooklyn Museum, Gift of Mrs. Robert G. Olmsted and Constable MacCracken, 65.239.8

3
The House of Pingat

THE HOUSE OF PINGAT

The name of Emile Pingat is almost totally unrecognized today, yet during the second half of the nineteenth century he was one of the most prominent French couturiers—revered especially by American clients, perhaps only second to Worth and at least as much as Laferrière. Many considered Pingat's creations the most select. Craftsmanship of the house can be deemed near-flawless, the epitome of the designing dressmaker's art, in which flashy fabrics are usually sublimated to subtle surface trims. His clothes, murmuring elegance rather than shouting affluence, demand close inspection inside and out.

Emile Pingat was a contemporary of Charles Frederick Worth; their careers and training ran parallel chronologically. Jean-Philippe Worth allows how "a certain M. Pingat, also an employee of a big firm, profited by my father's example" in setting up his own business.[1]

The name Pingat, like that of Worth, is not a common one in the Didot-Bottin Paris trade directories; in any given year there is but one of each. In 1855 a Mlle Pingat is listed as a corset maker at 371 rue Saint-Honoré; it is not known what, if any, was her relationship to the E. Pingat who appears in the 1860 directory as Pingat, Hudson et Cie at 30 rue Louis-le-Grand (a street running immediately parallel to the rue de la Paix), the address maintained by the firm well into the twentieth century. From the salons and workrooms there came "hautes nouveautés, confections pour dames, étoffes de soie unies et façonnies pour robes de ville, robes de bal, manteaux de cour, dentelles et guipures (magnificent fancy articles, ready-made clothing for women, plain and unique silk fabrics for town and day dresses, ball gowns, court trains, hand- and machine-made laces). By 1864 the name Hudson[2] has been dropped, and Pingat is on his own. Like Worth, Pingat is never the sole occupant of his building, and like his colleagues in the apparel industry, Pingat sells both custom-made and wholesale garments (fig. 3.1). We can only

Stamped gold on white petersham
c. 1863–68

speculate about the scope of Pingat's establishment, for like Worth, he merely promotes himself in the directories as purveyor of "nouveautés confectionées" (outfitter of fancy articles).

In 1896 Pingat, who apparently had no heirs or prospects interested in assuming his occupation, transferred his business to someone of a younger generation but of an already established dressmaking firm, A. Wallès & Cie. This move is documented in a small, obscure advertisement headlined "Letter from Paris":

> Pingat, who for so many years has made French taste dominant in Europe and America by his skills in clothing women in tasteful stuffs and graceful styles—Pingat has arrived at the knowledge that even success may become a burden when borne alone, and has determined to take a co-adjutor. With his usual good judgment, he has chosen M. Wallès, a true artist, "the right man for the right place," who will second the master's efforts by his youthful energy. With this infusion of new blood, combined with its excellent traditions, the house will continue to do all that it has hitherto done in demonstrating the superiority of French elegance on two continents.[3]

The wording suggests that Pingat was weary of supporting a nearly forty-year-old creative business that catered to the mercurial minds and manners of a sophisticated international clientele. Retirement perhaps seemed a sweet surcease from the demands that had propelled him to the near-pinnacle of his profession. This is the last we hear from Emile Pingat the dressmaker; between 1898 and 1900 an E. Pingat (profession unspecified) is listed in the Paris trade directory (Didot-Bottin) at 1 rue August-Vacquerie and in 1901–2 as a *rentier*, or retired person of independent means, at 19 rue Bassano. Thereafter the name Pingat ceases.

One quickly realizes how lucky Worth was to have sons to follow and assist in his declining years and what might have propelled the name Pingat forward if the situation had been similar. Instead, recognizing he could not crest the wave of up-and-coming designers such as Rouff and Paquin in the 1890s, Pingat relinquished his business to the careful if not brilliantly creative hands of M. Wallès.

Interestingly, the name Wallès first appears in the Paris directories in 1854 as an associate or partner of Maison Gagelin—operating from adjacent addresses at 84–90 rue Richelieu (1854–63). The assumption that Wallès is a textile dealer is borne out when in 1873–74 the Gagelin association is discontinued and the Wallès business, specializing in imported English fabrics, is relocated to 148 rue Montmartre. The breakup may not have been gainful for Wallès: in the following years, 1875–77, no Wallès is listed.[4] For the year 1878 a Mme Wallès advertises as a couturier at 8 rue de Choiseul, and in 1882 A. Wallès takes over the listing at that address, making dresses

3.1 (*Opposite*) Sketch of Pingat toilettes by A. Sandoz for *L'Illustration*, 1889.

and wraps.[5] For much of the decade Wallès additionally is making costumes for young girls and infants and in 1886 has an order to make clothes for the Austrian court; apparently by 1892 court dresses were a specialty of the house. When A. Wallès unites with Pingat in 1896, he gives up his 15 rue Auber address (1888–96), transferring his business and name to the 30 rue Louis-le-Grand premises occupied by Pingat; here he continues well into the twentieth century. The lasting status of the Wallès/Pingat house is reaffirmed by photographic and editorial inclusion in the exclusive fashion monthly *Les Modes* in the early twentieth century.

The importance of Pingat to English-speaking visitors to Paris may be judged from that bible of travel guides, Baedeker's. In the 1890–91 English edition, *Guide to Paris*, travelers are recommended to the three top Parisian haute couture houses: Worth, Pingat, and Laferrière.[6] Perhaps Baedeker's was unaware of the lively and vast network of ladies' letters, diaries, and fashion journals that offered opinions on all the Parisian shopping sites. In his widely distributed 1882 book on tailoring women's clothes, James McCall also interjects the names of Pingat and Worth, whom he considers two "of the three greatest artistic dressmakers in the World."[7]

While such evidence suggests the fame and stature of Maison Pingat, as yet we have no inkling of the spirit and temperament of the master behind the house and the designs as we do for Worth and Doucet. Nothing is known of the personality of M. Pingat, how he interacted with his peers and employees, what his clients thought of him and his creations, what his interests were, or what captivated his eye to be interpreted as a new fashion or decoration.

⧉◦⧇◦⧉◦⧇◦⧉◦⧇◦⧉◦⧇◦⧉

For a sense of the man, we can turn, above all, to the garments. As James McCall knowingly observed, Pingat, along with "every prominent dressmaker," had a unique set of dressmaking "rules," or formulas, by which his garments "can readily be distinguished."[8] McCall further stated, "The slightest variation by any workman would render him liable to instant discharge."[9]

From Pingat's first decade of activity, the 1860s, more formal evening gowns survive than do ephemeral Worths;[10] perhaps Pingat selected fabrics of greater stability. Right from the very beginning, about 1864, we have evidence of the skills of Pingat and what a creative and competitive force he must have been. Under the gold-stamped label of E. Pingat & Cie (see p. 177)

come two ethereal creamy white gowns, one satin and the other faille (fig. 3.2). Bold black Chantilly lace and narrow bands of cream Spanish blonde lace juxtaposed with gold-thread-balled black chenille fringe trim the bodice and form the three appliquéd funnel-shaped streamers of the skirt of the faille gown. As a companion outfit, probably acquired at the same time, the satin gown is ruched with silk tulle (now replaced) and has a bodice trimmed with a lattice, of looped gold-wrapped thread and gilt purling, which has been united by multicolored beads. From the lattice hang gilt bell flowerlike pendants. Interspersed among and anchoring the tulle are gilt-braid-edged looped tabs. These two remarkable evening dresses are from a New York family. In their time they were the equivalent of black gowns today— obligatory items in any fashionable wardrobe. Even before the decade of the 1860s ended, Pingat altered his label, enlarging his name and dropping "Cie." (See p. 182.) Client commitment was remarkably secure, as several extant garments from the 1860s would seem to have been acquired at least in pairs. Mrs. Charles (Annie H.) Carver went to Pingat about the time she was presented at the court of Napoleon III and Empress Eugénie in 1868. Now faded to a lavender from a brighter purple, one of her surviving faille dresses

3.2   Emile Pingat. *Evening Toilettes*, c. 1864. Left: plain silk slipper satin draped with silk tulle; machine-made silk blonde lace, gilt metallic bell flower drops, threads, and beads. Right: cream silk faille; machine-made Chantilly and silk blonde laces, gilt-foil spangles. The Metropolitan Museum of Art, Gift of Mary Pierrepont Beckwith, 69.33.1 and 69.33.12.

Stamped gold on white petersham
c. 1865–78

Stamped gold on white, gold on black
petersham
c. 1876–90

had a high-necked, long-sleeved bodice for less formal wear in addition to the ubiquitous low-necked sleeveless one for evening functions (Philadelphia Museum of Art, 38.18.5). Pearl-encrusted, tasseled gimps cascade as trim over the informal basque bodice and skirt, while the evening waist unfortunately has been stripped of its pearly trimmings. Mrs. Carver's other silk-faille Pingat is stark—lemon yellow, relieved only by a remarkable ruched, tightly looped fringe of self material from which the weft threads have been withdrawn to create the pile (Philadelphia Museum of Art, 38.18.2). Another Annie—Annie Fredericka Schuchardt (Mrs. Edward Leverich) of New York City—danced through her debutante days in a flounced ball gown from about 1869–71 of pink faille decorated with foliate-sprayed blond lace and dined in a pale lime green faille matched with a faded yellow-green bengaline (Museum of the City of New York; 63.185.8, 63.185.2). The latter dress carries a noticeably heavy, almost vulgar machine-embroidered tongue-shaped beading edged with Valenciennes lace. And Mrs. R. Stuyvesant of New York is said to have waltzed around in a pink satin gown highlighted with silk tulle applied in various grades and embroidered with a delicate chain of pansies, roses, and lilies of the valley (Museum of the City of New York, 61.193.1). The surface decorations of Pingat, as much as cut and more than fabric, separate his creations from Worth, who relied largely on fabrics to carry his creations.[11]

From the mid-1870s survive two day dresses from the wardrobe of Annie Carver. The earlier, from about 1874, is perhaps as beautifully conceived as it is finely executed (fig. 3.3). Unlike the sometimes slapdash products of Worth, this three-piece silk afternoon dress in navy bengaline and navy and tan taffeta and satin stripe is a lesson in the traditions of couture. From the careful selection of sharply contrasting fabric (smooth and ribbed, light and dark) to the attention to detail (finely felled seams worked in a most exacting manner), this garment is a masterpiece of creativity inside and out. Even the selection of trims should not go unnoticed; where a weakly designed and made blonde lace might have been used, Pingat has chosen instead a silk-floss machine-embroidered net that repeats in quite a surprising manner the stripes of the fabric. Broad, heart-shaped palmettes terminate the stripes of the front apron and back train of the overskirt. These emanate from an ogival central chain from which tri-clustered floral sprays spring on the other side. As a finishing to this application, two types of fringed tassels—one cream and one navy—interplay along the sawtooth edge of the leaves. The foot of the train is treated with novelty pleating. The second Carver dress, from about 1875–76, is much more severe in cut (Philadelphia Museum of Art, 38.18.8). Fabricated from ice blue silk crepe de chine, it has a long basque bodice, to which an overskirt of self material is attached. The matching body-giving silk faille underskirt is visible only at the hemline in front and in the back train.

3.3 Emile Pingat. *Reception Dress*, c. 1874. Stripes in silk satin and taffeta, plain silk bengaline; silk-floss-embroidered net. Worn by Mrs. Charles (Annie H.) Carver. Philadelphia Museum of Art, Gift of Mr. and Mrs. Ogden Wilkinson Headington in memory of Ogden D. Wilkinson, 38.18.12.

Again a complicated pleating—fanning knife pleats attached to box-pleated fingers—finishes the train foot. With its hipline polonaise and side-back drapery, this dress is of deliberate late seventeenth-century inspiration.

By 1880 Pingat was recognized as the master of outerwear: "For dressy jackets, Pingat (who is a great authority on mantles) is using basket woven clothes, combining several colors."[12] His exterior garments appealed to all who admired tailoring skills, once the realm of the English but much admired, adopted, and altered in mid-nineteenth-century Paris.

The English, in turn, admired one of Pingat's designs for the 1880 demi-season. Buyers from London's Lewis and Allenby brought back to the costume department a "principle novelty . . . the crinoline costume designed by Pingat, and intended to introduce a very decided crinoline to the fashionable world. The back is an entirely plain breadth, filled up by the flounced dress improver, and the amount of material incorporated in its voluminous folds is quite astonishing."[13] Reading further, one learns that the fabrics are greenish fawn-colored vicuna and plush to match—neither lightweight substances and certainly requiring a structured "dress improver'' for support. Dress improvers were reed, featherbone, fabric, and/or wire devices designed to support the back bustle configuration of the skirt. Sometimes they were built into the garment, as this instance would indicate. It is surmised that the smooth lines of the undraped skirt were supported by a soft bustle of gathered strips of starched cotton fabric; this system would give the semirounded back a little projecting shape; the front of the gown would have had a vertical tablier. In 1880 the fashion was for form-fitting but draped styles, with emphasis given to hip-hugging lines.

Maison Pingat citations in *The Queen* over a three-month period in 1882 give a valuable overall indication of the house's scope at the time.[14] For the summer were "some exquisitely fitting braided cloth jackets, in the English style; batiste skirts, embroidered in color with bodice to match; rich grenadine toilettes, broché with velvet flowers; embroidered crêpe de chine skirts mounted on moiré, and short foulard skirts spotted with large dots. Japanese cotton costumes, trimmed with coarse lace and short silk costumes are much made here, also cream surrah matinées [wraps] trimmed with lace and blue bows, all having the graceful Watteau plait at the back.'' For mid-summer, the house was "busy making costumes for country visits and déshabillés, or tea gowns. The latter are in black surrah, with a gathered Watteau plait at the back and opening in front over écru lace, ornamented with blue bows. For ordinary calling dresses much shot taffeta is used, and for the 'trotteuses' or walking costumes [with much-shortened hemlines] serge cloth; the skirts kilted [pleated] and machine stitched and the jacket bodices braided. The summer dresses in light Japanese cottons printed to imitate writings in Arabic characters are general but the embroidered écru batiste costumes turned out at this Maison are decidedly pretty." And as the Season approached—early to mid-winter—"they are busy over dinner, evening and château dresses. The materials are rich brocade, embossed velvet with satin ground, Ottoman velvet and broché plush on a thick repped ground." The trims were the expected Spanish blonde lace, gold thread embroidery, "grelot" (bell-shaped) buttons, flowers worked in shaded beads, and an unexpectedly pointed low evening bodice.

For young debutante clients and their sisters in 1883 there were summer costumes of veiling in such light colors as cream or ivory. The older generation was being richly dressed in pale blue brocatelle covered with pompadour flowers, cream satin, and the inevitable lace flounces.[15]

In the fashion press, adjectives such as "pretty," "rich," "chefs d'oeuvre," and "beautiful" generally precede descriptions of Pingat toilettes; as opposed to less enthusiastic personal or editorial perceptions about Worth, such raves abound in a review of 1885: "There were many mantles and Pingat's mantles are chefs d'oeuvre and there was a tea gown likewise from the same house which deserves special mention. It was of cream broché satin,

3.4   Emile Pingat. *Evening Ensemble*, composed of two bodices and one skirt, c. 1885. Blue-black plain silk velvet embroidered with metallic stylized flowers; coordinating embroidered net, machine-made Chantilly lace. Worn by Mrs. Charles A. Roebling. Philadelphia Museum of Art, Gift of Mrs. Carroll S. Tyson, 49.29.3.

the design being pines, outlined in small green leaves and flowerettes and trimmed with gold braid and shaded green beads. In front, from the throat to the feet, there was drapery of twine-colored gauze worked in green and gold. There was a cream Sicilienne mantle, bordered with emu feathers, and another of bright steel gauze, very effective and novel with the latter there was a muff to match.''[16]

Pingat's eye for detail and control of seemingly discordant materials is readily seen in a magnificent three-piece dress, which must have been made for wintertime evening functions about 1885 (fig. 3.4). There are two

Woven metallic gold on white, pink on white,
black on white, metallic silver on white,
metallic silver on black, gold on black
c. 1885–95

bodices—one low-necked and sleeveless, the other high and sleeved—and an imaginatively asymmetrically draped skirt. The body of the ensemble is deep midnight blue plain velvet, to which is melded black net embroidered in gold and silver threads. The embroidery falls over onto the velvet and is graduated in scale appropriate to its placement on the garment. The motif is an impression of a carnation.

Making an uncharacteristically delicate statement in the mid-1880s is a two-piece afternoon dress that belonged to Mrs. C. Goodhue of 189 Madison Avenue, New York City (Museum of the City of New York, 50.300.1). The supporting and trim fabric is Prussian blue bengaline, over which is draped a silk crepe printed with hummingbirds darting among small botanicals. Almost impressionistic, the birds are in maroon, blues, olive, and grayed pinks on a deep cream ground.

What the tulip or the bluette was to Worth, the poppy was to Pingat in the 1880s and 1890s. In one of the most evocative interpretations of nascent Art Nouveau motifs applied to a garment, we find poppies rippling over a dolman opera wrap (fig. 3.5). It is ivory-colored satin with appliqué pile floral-blossom cutouts secured with silk floss in a raised loop and with gilt metallic thread, which is looped around the floss; the embroidery treatment recalls the napped texture of poppy petals. White fox fur edges the high, round neckline and continues down the center front, while cream-colored marabou edges the trumpet-shaped cuffs and thigh-length hemline. Another wrap of almost identical thigh-length cut, but lacking the pizzazz, has the same fur trim, used now on all edges (Victoria and Albert Museum, T64.1976). While the fabric is patterned—a white silk faille patterned with a cut pile and satin feather plume—the impression is of overall whiteness, with shape and interest lost. Surely the clients who succumbed to these wraps must have considered price when making their purchases, as one garment is truly memorable and the other boringly prosaic.

In another instance of the poppy motif, an unadorned but patterned fabric fairly shouts at observers. Rows of crimson poppies in uncut pile bend on the black satin ground of a reception gown whose machine-made black Spanish blonde lace trim gives it a vaguely Iberian quality (Philadelphia Museum of Art, 49.29.2).

Extant garments suggest that in the 1880s and 1890s more and more clients sought out Pingat for his wraps—some memorable, some mundane. Of the former, two from the Museum of Fine Arts, Boston, deserve mention. One is a full-length dolman wrap of cream wool twilled flannel patterned with cumulus clouds centered in a golden-thread sunburst (52.1145). The second, a hip-length dolman, is a brass-colored silk plush and dark brown velvet encrusted with embroidered intertwining paisley, or *buta*, shapes, which are worked in an unusual combination of textural silk twists and fine wool yarns

(1972.911). A characteristic of Pingat wraps of the late 1880s to early 1890s is the elongated-shaped front pendant, which is reminiscent of those of 1830s pelerines but which he has updated with trapezoidal ends (pls. 36, 37). A jacket from about 1893 shows Near Eastern influences, here pseudo–Egyptian (pls. 39, 40). Again velvet—brownish black—serves as the background, to which twisted cording in blue, white, and tomato, and white and mauve has been couched, along with olive chenille thread. Repeating motifs include the Eastern stylized carnation, broad heart-shaped leaves, and stylized versions of unfurling foliate forms. Occasionally motifs are so close to Worth as to make the creations of the two houses almost indistinguishable; examples are a cape with applied bead and cord peacock plumes (pl. 38a) and a dolman-cape wrap of steam-embossed steel gray silk velvet in a scale design appliquéd with bold cord and bead passementerie and fringe (Wadsworth Atheneum, Hartford, 39.673). Worth, however, would probably have made a bolder statement with the peacock motif and selected a more sharply defined voided velvet for the other wrap. Two capes—one shoulder, one thigh-length—are perhaps some of the house's most interesting garments from Emile Pingat's last days there in the first half of the 1890s. One cape incorporates a decorated shoulder pelerine, which ends with "Eiffel Tower points" in front (pl. 38b). The eye and mind are captivated by the geometrized feather plumes; the motif carries an almost Aboriginal design quality reflective of the world's growing interest in colonial cultures. In its bold starkness of applied design, this wrap is totally unrelated to the then-prevalent design vocabulary of naturalistic floral and entomological specimens. And finally, there remains an elbow-length colette, which is without the deadly heaviness of most such 1890s jet-beaded creations; instead it is light, almost frivolous. The fabric is a milk-chocolate silk bengaline, which has been box-pleated in radiating pointed tabs, with the two layers of tabs receiving a different beaded motif. Irregularly imposed seventeenth-century-style strapwork enhances the aura of lightness created through beadwork.

Although Pingat continued to receive press in the 1890s, the old enthusiasm was gone or diluted to words like "distingué," and more space was devoted to his construction techniques than to the visual aspects of a dress. Most extant garments also speak of a declining prowess and loss of verve. Among Pingat's last interesting toilettes still to be seen are a reception dress in a seventeenth-century manner fitted for Mrs. Robert Treat Paine (née Lydia Williams Lyman) in about 1888 (pl. 33) and a modified eighteenth-century riding outfit possibly made for Emily Roebling or one of her numerous in-laws (pl. 35). Velvets full of body and ever gracefully draping are the primary fabrics of these two garments. On the Roebling outfit is to be seen the metallic embroidery so characteristic of the house.

3.5 Emile Pingat. *Dolman Opera Mantle*. Metallic-thread-appliquéd pile poppy flowers on ivory silk satin; white fox. The Metropolitan Museum of Art, Gift of Mrs. Howard Crosby Brokaw, 60.42.13.

Woven gold on bright blue
c. 1890–96

A greater variety of label configurations is associated with Pingat than with Worth. By 1874 the gilt-stamped labels of Pingat's cream silk moiré petersham carried "Paris" as well as the house's name and address (see p. 182). Around 1885 Pingat began to use a standard but variously colored woven label for outer garments (see p. 186) that would last until Wallès added his name in 1896 (see p. 189). There appears to have been only one brief break from this identification, around 1890, when Pingat tried at least one version of semi-Gothic, almost Art Nouveau calligraphy, in a very bright gold silk thread woven on an equally bright blue ground (see p. 188). For dresses he continued to use the previously described stamped versions.

⊰∘⊱⊰∘⊱⊰∘⊱⊰∘⊱

Just as information concerning Pingat is far sparser than the abundant material on Worth, so is much less known about Pingat's clients. By and large, his ladies seem to have been a more adventuresome lot than those who flocked to Worth.[17] Pingat clients were not merely showpieces, women on pedestals, whose role was to represent their husbands' wealth; many were achievers in their own right.[18]

Remarkably little garment evidence of Pingat—generally outerwear—survives in French collections to give us information about French clients. An article in *The Queen* tells us what was ordered for one French mademoiselle's 1885 trousseau:

> Pingat has been especially busy with wedding orders, an extensive one being for Mlle de Bravura, who was quite recently married in England. More than a dozen dresses were ordered from him, and very cleverly did he execute the command, for each one had a distinctive style, and in its way was decidedly attractive.
>
> The ballgowns were beautiful—a pink satin, brocaded with small silver feathers, the tulle front spangled with silver, and sprays of honeysuckle festooning the drapery was decidedly pretty. Also one in yellow Sicilenne, the shade called "beurre frais" but even fresh butter varies in tone, and the exact hue is difficult to describe; it was, however, in this instance a beautiful shade and was embroidered with silver marguerites and trimmed with trails of Banksia roses. A white satin brocaded with flowers in a gold thread, the tablier embroidered gold gauze draped with dark blue campanulas; a pale blue satin brocade,

trimmed with gold and ficelle, lace and roses, and a visiting dress consisting of a brown satin underskirt, with a brown and blue broché overdress tied in front with ribbons of the two colors, were all in excellent taste.[19]

The evidence gathered through existing garments indicates that clients from North America predominated. From Boston, New York, Philadelphia, Chicago, San Francisco, and other cities women sought the services of Maison Pingat. Already mentioned was Annie Carver, of the Philadelphia area, a regular client for at least the better part of a decade (1868–78). She was socially prominent enough to have found herself at the court of Napoleon III and Eugénie in 1868 with a wardrobe containing several Pingats (Philadelphia Museum of Art, 38.18.2,.5,.6,.8,.12) (see fig. 3.3).

Distaff members of the brilliant Roebling engineering family also chose Pingat. Mrs. Charles A. Roebling and Emily Warren Roebling (Mrs. Washington Auguste Roebling) both found the velvets, metallic embroideries, and historical interpretations of Pingat to their taste (pl. 35). Emily may have favored an eighteenth-century look and Mrs. Charles a seventeenth-century one, but the garments of both speak of straightforward, extremely elegant women who understood beauty and structure in everyday application. Emily, who oversaw the completion of the Brooklyn Bridge following her husband's near-fatal accident at the site, would have been particularly aware of such design principles.

In Boston, Mrs. Henry Adams, wife of the illustrious American historian, author, and statesman, covered up an old gold brocade and velvet Worth evening dress purchased in 1879 with an evening cloak "made by Pingat and quite the 'utter'" in 1882.[20]

Mrs. Augustus Newland Eddy, one of the prettiest and most prominent of Chicago's mercantile Society, stopped at Pingat during a European excursion with her father in 1878. There she placed an order for a dress for the first Mrs. Marshall Field, a cloak for her sister Dell (Delia Spencer married first Arthur J. Caton, and later Marshall Field of merchandising fame), and one for herself. Returning three days later, she succumbed to a "party dress." In another four days she was told her dress would be fitted on Thursday. This gown must have been a personal favorite: she wears it in a family-portrait photograph taken after her return and in her portrait (fig. 3.6) painted by George Peter Alexander Healy (1813–1894). When her friend Frances Macbeth Glessner, a lady of strong independent tastes whose H. H. Richardson Renaissance-revival house was furnished with Arts and Crafts decor, set off for Europe in 1890, she carried Mrs. Eddy's recommendations for Doucet, Dusuzeau, and "*Pingat* rue Louis le Grand—ask for Madame Blanche—she is perfectly reliable—all materials and fitter of first class. Dresses and cloaks."[21]

Woven pale blue on white
c. 1896 on

189

3.6 Mrs. Augustus Newland Eddy's (née Abbie Louise Spencer) Pingat "party" dress ordered Sept. 17, 1878, and her portrait by George Peter Alexander Healy (1813–1894). Chicago Historical Society, Gifts of Albert J. Beveridge III, dress, 1976.270.1; painting, 1979.54.

3.7 (*Opposite*) Mrs. Leland Stanford in a Worth gown with a Pingat wrap draped on the chair as portrayed by Léon-Joseph Florentin Bonnat (1833–1922) in 1881. Stanford University Museum, 12020.

A Pingat garment also appears in a very regal full-length portrait of Jane Lathrop Stanford (Mrs. Leland Stanford) of California painted by Léon-Joseph Florentin Bonnat (1833–1922) in 1881 (fig. 3.7). She stands formally attired in a Worth gown, and her right hand rests on a draped Pingat mantle. Mrs. Stanford may well have acquired the garments reproduced in her portrait during an 1880 trip to Paris. As an energetic helpmate, she rarely left the side of her determined husband; through the tragic loss of their only son, they were further united in the project of establishing and constructing in Palo Alto a university in his memory.

Recognizable names on a short list of Pingat clients would include Mrs. Walter Lippincott, ladies of the Pierrepont and Hewitt families, and Mrs. William H. Vanderbilt. To the end, Society found uses for the garments of Pingat. In the 1890s a few New York girls participated in a fad of modeling for sketch artists, dressed in millinery from the top Parisian hat maker Virot and in Pingat wraps, coats, jackets, capelets, and mantles. The seventy-five cents an hour they earned was passed on to charity.[22]

⊰⊱◦⊰⊱◦⊰⊱◦⊰⊱◦⊰⊱

Plate 33 Emile Pingat. *Reception Dress*, c. 1888. Silk velvet and brocade; lace trim. Worn by Mrs. Robert Treat Paine (née Lydia Williams Lyman). Museum of Fine Arts, Boston, Gift of Mr. Henry S. Hall, Jr., 56.849

Plates 34, 35 Emile Pingat. *Promenade Costume*, c. 1888. Silk velvet with metallic-silver-thread embroidery. Probably worn by Mrs. Washington Auguste Roebling (née Emily Warren). The Brooklyn Museum, Anonymous Gift in memory of Mrs. John Roebling, 70.53.1

Plates 36, 37 Emile Pingat. *Dolman*, c. 1891. Wool-face cloth; appliquéd silk velvet, ostrich-feather trim. The Brooklyn Museum, Gift of Cornelia Gracie Henshaw, 64.117.6

Plate 38a Emile Pingat. *Cape*, c. 1891. Silk velvet with embroidered peacock-feather trim. Worn by Mrs. Frederick Augustus Constable (née Louise Bolmer). The Brooklyn Museum, Gift of Mrs. Robert G. Olmsted and Constable MacCracken, 65.239.15

Plate 38b Emile Pingat. *Cape*, c. 1891. Wool broadcloth; embroidered with cording and beads, mink trim. Work by the Misses Marion and/or Madeleine Litchfield. The Brooklyn Museum, Gift of Miss Marion Litchfield, 50.72.32

Plates 39, 40 Emile Pingat. *Jacket*, c. 1893. Silk velvet and satin, corded appliqué embroidery. Worn by the Misses Marion and/or Madeleine Litchfield. The Brooklyn Museum, Gift of Miss Marion Litchfield, 50.72.13

NOTES

1 The House of Worth

The House

1 Hollander 1978, p. 356.
2 Hooper 1892, p. 67.
3 An opera cloak of about 1895 in the Museum of London (76.10) carries the labels: "Lewis & Allenby/Cloak Makers to the Queen/Regent Street" and "Conduit St. W.," and the Worth wrap signature label, brown on white.
4 In the Paris trade directories (Didot-Bottin) there is a clear delineation of the name status of the business conducted by Gagelin at 93 rue de Richelieu. (In other sources, the business is inconsistently referred to as Gagelin-Opigez or Opigez.) In 1830 Gagelin-Versepuy offer "nouveautés, câchemires de l'Inde et Française, Merinos, étoffes de fantaisie, robes de bal, corbeilles de mariage, blondes de soie, et broderies" (fancy goods, Indian and French cashmere shawls, woolen goods, novelty yard goods, ball gowns, wedding presents, articles of silk lace, and embroidered articles). By 1840 Gagelin et Opigez (Ancienne Maison Versepuy) operate at this address, offering silks and shawls. In 1847 the business is styled Opigez, Chazelle et Cie and there is no main entry for Gagelin, found only under Opigez in the nouveautés section, again in alliance with Versepuy. In about 1850 the company assumes the address of 83 rue Richelieu.
5 Their shawls and silks were exhibited in Class 23.
6 *The Times*, March 12, 1895.
7 Worth was never the sole occupant or owner of the building.
8 At this time rue de la Paix was of little fashion consequence. However, its aura was to change with the building of the newly commissioned Paris Opera.
9 The same range of goods is enumerated on an 1857 billhead.
10 Hegermann-Lindencrone 1912, p. 90.
11 Bobergh did not marry until 1872, and then it was to a fellow Swede, the actress Thérèse Börklund.
12 Hegermann-Lindencrone 1912, p. 96.
13 See Museum of the City of New York (35.365.3), for such a color combination.
14 Hegermann-Lindencrone 1912, p. 189.
15 *Felice* may be a misspelling for *Felix*. de Marly 1980b, p. 45.
16 Adburgham 1961, p. 54.
17 Hegermann-Lindencrone 1912, p. 48, pp. 34–35.
18 *Harper's Bazar*, Dec. 23, 1871, p. 820.
19 The expense code utilized by the house has yet to be broken. de Marly 1980b offers an analysis based on the phrase *Chers Frères Worth, on gagne Dieu mais avec volonté-reflechissez*, where each first letter assumes a numerical counterpart from 1 to 0. However, missing from this phrase is the letter *B*, which appears with considerable frequency in the model portfolios.
20 Latour 1958, p. 90.
21 *All the Year Round*, Feb. 1863. Twenty years later the same observation was made in *The Queen*, Aug. 11, 1883.
22 Richardson 1971, p. 241.
23 Quoted in ibid.
24 Tharp 1965, p. 41.
25 de Marly 1980a, p. 101.
26 Adams Letters, p. 223.
27 *Harper's Bazar*, March 23, 1893, p. 226.
28 Latour 1958, p. 92.
29 Quoted in Richardson 1971, p. 240.
30 Adolphus 1895, p. 189.
31 *The Englishwoman's Domestic Magazine*, Sept. 1871, pp. 290–91.
32 Ibid.
33 Ibid., July and Aug. 1871, pp. 123, 373.
34 *The Queen*, Feb. 21, 1885, p. 195.
35 Ross 1963, p. 251.
36 Worth 1928, p. 171.
37 Hilaire Belloc, in *The Ladies' Realm*, 1896.
38 *Kelly's Postal Directory* 1903.
39 Poiret 1931, p. 65.
40 Ibid., p. 67.
41 *American Tailor and Cutter*, Oct. 1897, p. 63.
42 *Femina*, Jan. 1, 1903, supplement.

The Worth Men

1 Parisian fashion has not been the exclusive dominion of the French. Some of the most brilliant practitioners have been foreigners, including Englishmen Worth and Charles James.
2 Hooper 1892, p. 67.
3 de Marly 1980b, p. 56.
4 *All the Year Round*, Feb. 28, 1863, p. 9.
5 *Harper's Bazar*, March 23, 1895, p. 226.

6   Sala 1948, vol. 2, p. 327.
7   Adams Letters, p. 183.
8   Client from 1867 to July 1895, when she deserted the house for the newer, up-and-coming firm of Paquin.
9   *Harper's Bazar*, March 23, 1895, p. 226.
10 Evidential findings point to at least another daughter, Anne Marie, and the possibility of up to three more offspring by Jean-Philippe.
11 About 1900 Gaston Worth demolished the complex, replacing it with a villa of his own that likewise has been overshadowed.
12 Richardson 1971, p. 241.
13 Hooper 1892, p. 67.
14 Goncourt, as quoted in de Marly 1980b, p. 204.
15 de Marly 1980b, p. 203.
16 Adolphus 1895, pp. 183–85.
17 Ibid., pp. 187–88.
18 Metternich, as quoted in de Marly 1980b, p. 198.
19 Goncourt, as quoted in de Marly 1980b, p. 200.
20 *Harper's Bazar*, March 23, 1895, p. 226.
21 The above philosophy had been remarked to François Cartier, the jeweler, who later would be united to the Worth family by marriage.
22 Worth 1928, p. 179.
23 de Marly 1980b, p. 206.
24 Melba 1925, pp. 154–55.
25 Worth 1928, p. vi.
26 Ibid., pp. 74, 76.
27 *Harper's Bazar*, Oct. 29, 1898, p. 937.
28 Poiret 1931, pp. 66–67.

Distribution

1   Carette 1889, p. 177.
2   Adolphus 1895, p. 190.
3   In nineteenth-century France the meaning of *modiste* was different from that applied in English-speaking countries. *Modiste* meant a milliner, never a dressmaker—which was one of the first lessons to be learned by luxury-seeking American women coming to Paris for a gown. See *Harper's Bazar*, Nov. 9, 1895, p. 903.
4   *The Englishwoman's Domestic Magazine*, Dec. 1, 1870, p. 354.
5   Ibid., 1871, p. 366.
6   Ibid., July 1872, p. 119.
7   Ibid., Sept. 1, 1870.
8   Ibid., Sept. 1, 1871, p. 306.
9   Goncourt, as quoted in de Marly 1980b, p. 140.
10 Worth additionally did stage clothes for the plays of Alexandre Dumas, dressing, for instance, Mlle Blanche Pierson for the 1880 production of *Père Prodigue*.
11 *The Queen*, Dec. 4, 1880, p. 509.
12 *Harper's Bazar*, June 22, 1895, p. 495.

13 In Great Britain and the United States, the majority of late nineteenth- and early twentieth-century dressmakers were of Irish extraction or selected an Irish name, if they did not adopt a French one.
14 *Harper's Bazar*, June 29, 1895, p. 515.
15 Ibid., Nov. 12, 1891, cover, p. 916.
16 Ibid., Jan. 16, 1892, cover, p. 51.
17 *Vogue*, June 10, 1893, supplement.

Designs

1   In the same way it should be remembered that all black nineteenth-century garments were not set aside for, or associated with, periods of mourning.
2   *Harper's Bazar*, Nov. 8, 1873, p. 716.
3   *The Queen*, May 15, 1880, p. 431.
4   Ibid., Oct. 15, 1881, p. 379.
5   *The Ladies' Treasury*, Oct. 1881, p. 646.
6   Hegermann-Lindencrone 1914, p. 93.
7   *The Queen*, Feb. 26, 1881, p. 203.
8   For further discussion see Appendix on Worth labels.
9   *Harper's Bazar*, Nov. 8, 1890, p. 871.
10 Ibid., Dec. 24, 1892, p. 1043.
11 Tradition has it that the velvet fabric was woven by the Cheney firm of Manchester, Ct., and exported to France for making up and that it was copied from a portrait of La Grande Mlle, sister of Louis XIV.
12 *Harper's Bazar*, Nov. 22, 1890, p. 911. This description can be related to Hewitt suit jackets at The Brooklyn Museum (31.62, 31.30).
13 *Harper's Bazar*, Oct. 10, 1891, cover.
14 These photographic albums are divided between the Victoria and Albert Museum collection and the Museum of Costume, Bath. The two sets are not mutually exclusive, and within the sets there is considerable repetition of models. It is the opinion of the author that these volumes are not the chronological record that their bindings would indicate.
15 Sandoz's sketches of Worth garments appeared from at least 1888 to 1898 in *The Queen*, *Revue de la mode*, and *Harper's Bazar*.
16 The association with the historical document was made by Janet Arnold, who has included the example in Arnold 1985, pp. 36–37, 97.
17 For fancy dresses, two can be identified with portraits: Cabanel's Venetian Princess was used for Mrs. William K. Vanderbilt in 1883 and Mrs. Calvin Brice appeared at the 1897 Bradley Martin ball as Velázquez's Infanta Margarita.
18 *Harper's Bazar*, Sept. 5, 1891, p. 671.
19 Millar 1963, pls. 72, 80.
20 The creation of Mrs. Eddy's garment was supervised by her vendeuse at Worth, Mme Deve, while her sister's vendeuse, Mme Bond,

oversaw the work for Catherine's dress. This division of authority was only natural as Catherine's aunt, Mrs. Arthur Caton (née Delia Spencer, later Mrs. Marshall Field), was giving the dress to her niece. According to family tradition, the gowns were made in competition to see which would be the most exquisitely turned out; no result is recorded. The Chicago Historical Society owns another Worth—a fancy dress (1976.270.6) said to have been inspired by a Nattier portrait. This time, it was Mrs. Eddy who wished to assume the appearance of Mme Pompadour.

21 *Harper's Bazar*, Feb. 9, 1895, p. 109.
22 The archives are an amalgam of Worth and Paquin materials, and it is assumed that the watercolored models are all Worth designs. However, the origin of pencil-drawn skirt sketches from the late 1860s to early 1870s is conjectured to be Worth. Fashion plates extracted from their publications could have served both houses.
23 This association was brought to my attention through the kindness of Françoise Tetart-Vittu of the Musée de la Mode et du Costume, Paris.
24 The late costume historian Yvonne Deslandres claimed in a 1979 exhibition catalogue, *La Grande Jetée*, that Janet produced designs for Worth, even though she makes no direct connection.
25 The correlation was made in de Marly 1980b, for the sketch and Metternich photograph.
26 J.-P. Worth went on to say that present fashions had a tendency to be more and more utilitarian and he saw the "lady" of the twentieth century as one who would realize it was her duty to look her best under all circumstances and not to follow blindly the dictates of fashion.
27 *Vogue*, Aug. 1893, p. 8.
28 Ibid., Oct. 1893, p. 4.
29 Ibid., June 1893, p. 8.
30 In Blum 1974, p. 248.

Textiles, Trims, and Techniques

1 *The Ladies' Treasury*, March 1882, p. 224.
2 Worth 1928, p. 80.
3 *The Queen*, May 28, 1881, p. 539.
4 Ibid., Feb. 12, 1881, p. 159.
5 Ibid., Jan. 21, 1882, p. 51.
6 Ibid., Feb. 12, 1881, p. 159.
7 *The Ladies' Treasury*, Feb. 1883, p. 164.
8 *The Queen*, April 14, 1883, p. 315.
9 Ibid., Oct. 30, 1880, p. 387.
10 The Brooklyn Museum, 31.24: 38.7 cm repeat, 64 cm selvedge to selvedge. Museum of the City of New York, 41.224.3: 28.6 cm repeat, 64 cm selvedge to selvedge. Victoria and Albert

Museum Worth Archives, model no. 45046.
11 Museum of Fine Arts, Boston, 51.321: 15.6 cm repeat. Museum of the City of New York, unaccessioned: 15 cm repeat.
12 (Feathers) Storch and Martin 1889, opp. p. 56. (Gladiola) opp. p. 24 and Musée Historique des Tissus, Lyon, 24.997. (Phlox) opp. p. 28 and Musée Historique des Tissus, 24.998. (Roses) 25.009. (Lilacs) 25.004.
13 Musée Historique des Tissus, Lyon, 24.859, 60 cm selvedge to selvedge, 68 cm repeat.
14 Museum of the City of New York, unaccessioned: 60.5 cm selvedge to selvedge, 39 cm repeat.
15 The Metropolitan Museum of Art, 40.92.2: 69.5 cm selvedge to selvedge, 29.5 cm repeat. Cooper-Hewitt Museum, 1969.125.1: 64.5 cm selvedge to selvedge, 108 cm repeat.
16 *Harper's Bazar*, Nov. 1873.
17 *The Queen*, Oct. 21, 1882, p. 375.
18 Ibid., Oct. 29, 1881, p. 429.
19 *The Ladies' Treasury*, June 1881, p. 344.
20 A small number are trimmed with appliqués on a net ground, and replacement or additional laces were not calculated.
21 Two sample cards are in The Brooklyn Museum, and none of the samples match with a lace used on Worth gowns in the Hewitt collection.
22 One of the earliest known instances of the house reinterpreting a textile and garment from an earlier period or different culture is a dolman mantle, possibly a *sortie de bal* constructed from a Moroccan jellaba of clear blue silk ottoman highlighted with beige and metallic silver and finished with fringe of blue and silver (Musée de la Mode et du Costume, Paris, 62.208.120).
23 *The Domestic Monthly*, Oct. 1, 1889, p. 28.
24 *Vogue*, Jan. 4, 1894, supplement.
25 While it is not known if Worth was the first to put elements of the inside on the outside, many twentieth-century designers have followed the tradition, each assuming he was the first to do so.

Clients

1 Hegermann-Lindencrone 1912, pp. 100–102.
2 Adams Letters, p. 183.
3 Ibid.
4 Oliphant 1878.
5 Sherwood 1884a, p. 118.
6 See pls. 10, 11, fig. 1.36. The variation in dimensions would seem to be related to garment function rather than date, as the two garments cited, both Worths, date from different decades and generations. One is from the mid-1890s, and the other from the mid-1860s.

7 Hooper 1892, p. 67.

8 *Peterson's Magazine*, Nov. 1865, pp. 358–60.

9 Burnett 1880, p. 16.

10 Fawcett 1881, p. 191.

11 Wharton 1920, p. 257.

12 Adolphus 1895, p. 194.

13 Sherwood 1884b.

14 Born Lillie Greenough of Cambridge, Mass., she married first Charles Moulton and later the Dane Johan Hegermann-Lindencrone. Her first Worths were acquired, as a bride, in 1863 at age nineteen.

15 Hegermann-Lindencrone 1912, pp. 279–81.

16 Adolphus 1895, p. 194.

17 Sherwood 1884b.

18 Worth 1928, p. 143.

19 *Harper's Bazar*, March 23, 1895, p. 226.

20 *Vogue*, March 15, 1894, p. 102.

21 Ibid., Aug. 10, 1893, supplement.

22 Article source unknown, dated Feb. 1883, The Metropolitan Museum of Art, New York, Costume Institute, vertical files.

23 Tharp 1965, p. 43.

24 Adams Letters, p. 180.

25 Ibid., p. 223.

26 Ibid., p. 352.

27 Lynes 1981, p. 19.

28 Ibid.

29 It is not known who might have been the wearer of some of the more youthful and diminutive gowns from the turn of the century, as Amy's daughter, the Princess Viggo, was born in 1895.

30 Worth 1928, p. 223.

31 Beerbohm 1896, p. 52.

32 Hooper 1892, p. 67.

33 *The Englishwoman's Domestic Magazine*, vol. 10, 1871, p. 231.

34 She had been Princess Dagmar of Denmark, younger sister of Alexandra, princess of Wales, before she was betrothed into the Russian royal family, first to Grand Duke Nicholas and, on his death, to his younger brother Alexander, who became czar.

35 Lonergan 1907, p. 199.

36 *The Ladies' Treasury*, Feb. 1883, p. 165, and *The Queen*, Jan. 27, 1883, p. 79.

37 Worth 1928, p. 51.

38 *The Ladies' Treasury*, Feb. 1883, p. 164.

39 Ibid., Jan. 1879, p. 44.

40 Paget 1923, p. 237.

41 Worth 1928, p. 205.

42 *The Queen*, Jan. 7, 1882, p. 5.

43 Lonergan 1907, p. 200.

44 Worth 1928, p. 117.

45 *The Queen*, Nov. 24, 1883, p. 597.

46 Ibid., May 27, 1882, p. 455.

47 Worth 1928, p. 115.

48 Hooper 1892, p. 67.

49 *The Queen*, Feb. 26, 1881, p. 203.

50 Ibid. and March 12, 1881, p. 244.

51 Worth 1928, passim.

52 See section on Distribution for further analysis.

53 *The Queen*, July 9, 1881, p. 45.

54 Hegermann-Lindercrone 1914, p. 274.

55 Nicolson 1977, p. 78.

56 Paget 1923, p. 195.

57 Worth 1928, pp. 100–101.

58 de Marly 1980b, p. 73.

59 Paget 1923, p. 320.

60 Ibid., p. 45.

61 Dorsey 1986, p. 127 (quoted from a 1905 issue of the *Paris Herald*).

62 Melba 1925, p. 55.

63 Ibid., p. 38.

64 Worth 1928, p. 170.

65 *L'Art et la mode*, Nov. and Dec. 1883, and *The Queen*, Dec. 16, 1882/83, p. 583.

66 Sichel 1958, p. 202.

67 Hilaire Belloc, in *The Ladies' Realm*, 1896.

68 *Vogue*, July 1893, supplement.

Appendix: *Worth Labels*

1 Fortelling the future construction of the dressmaker's labels is at least one woven example configured in the same outline as the stamped examples. It is to be found in a c. 1873 dress (The Brooklyn Museum, 33.74).

2 The configuration of this label is easily confused with that employed by the House of Rouff, also laid out with three similarly shaped elliptical forms, the central one containing the signature picked in garnet silk threads but rendered in an imitative manner (see p. 98).

3 Measurements from the petersham waistbands are only approximate, as two distorting elements make precise calculations impossible: the securing cross-stitches, which usually attach the band to the construction bones of the garment, pucker up the band; and the stress applied by the wearer may have stretched the band. In every grouping there were a few labels judged to be authentic to a particular garment that had measurements outside those listed above.

4 It is hard to tell if these were labels woven specifically for this purpose or if the signature segment was snipped from the longer label (see p. 34).

5 See pp. 84, 85, 88, 89.

6 Two coats, dated to c. 1905, carried only four digits, each beginning with *4*.

7 Not all garments related to specific clients bear numbered tags, and it might easily be speculated that these unnumbered garments were export or non-couture models. Pieces belonging to French clients are also unmarked.

8 Research was not conducted on garments from after 1905. The 1906 figure is a projection.

2 The House of Doucet

The Doucet Family Businesses

1   *Vogue*, Dec. 15, 1915, p. 54.
2   These directories, under various titles, were researched for the period 1815–1904. Not all editions were available.
3   Latour 1958, p. 137.
4   Chapon 1984, p. 39.
5   Ibid.
6   Ibid., p. 41.
7   Ibid.
8   Ibid., p. 42.
9   Ibid.
10   Articles sold were women's garments for at-home use, especially in the informal morning hours, petticoats and underskirts, bodices and informal jackets, short jackets, suites of clothes, preboxed garments, and infants' clothes.

The House

1   *Vogue*, Dec. 15, 1915, p. 54.
2   Ibid., Jan. 1, 1923, p. 196.
3   *Harper's Bazar*, Oct. 5, 1895, p. 799.
4   Ibid., Oct. 12, 1895, p. 819.
5   Ibid., Nov. 9, 1895, p. 903. With its four-yard-long court train and the excision of the high neck, the dress was readily recycled as a court-presentation gown. Balsan 1952, p. 96.
6   Chapon 1984, pp. 58–9.

Jacques Doucet

1   Chapon 1984, pp. 15–16.

2   *Bulletin de la Société de l'Histoire du Costume* 1 (1907–9): 33, 128.
3   In 1972 the Parisian auction house, Hôtel Drouot, would again sell Doucet possessions, this time the remains of his studio in the rue Saint-James, Neuilly.
4   Berger 1982, pp. 46–48.
5   His renowned art libraries, which still carry the Doucet name, are now at the University of Paris.
6   Gramont 1952, p. 73.
7   Chapon 1984, p. 23.

Designs

1   *Harper's Bazar*, April 2, 1892, p. 263.
2   Ibid., Aug. 17, 1895, p. 654.
3   Ibid., Nov. 23, 1895, p. 947.
4   Ibid., Oct. 5, 1895, p. 799.
5   Ibid., Sept. 21, 1895, p. 759.
6   Ibid., Jan. 5, 1895, p. 3.
7   Ibid., June 22, 1895, p. 495.
8   Ibid., Aug. 17. 1895, p. 654.
9   Ibid., June 29, 1895, p. 515.

Clients

1   Porel *Fils de Réjane, 1895–1920*, Paris, 1951, passim.
2   Pougy, as quoted in Chapon 1984, p. 67. Author's translation.
3   Some of her garments are found in the Musée de la Mode et du Costume, Paris.
4   Jachimowicz 1978, p. 48.
5   Wharton 1905, pp. 82–83.
6   *Harper's Bazar*, Aug. 31, 1895, p. 699.

3 The House of Pingat

1 Worth 1928, p. 23.

2 Of Hudson—a very Anglican name, like Worth—nothing more has been traced.

3 *Harper's Bazar*, Jan. 9, 1897, p. 42.

4 A business paid for each entry in Didot-Bottin, and an entry could be missing because of financial reasons, closure of business, or failure to meet the publishing deadline, which was October of the year preceding the date of publication.

5 An 1882 bridesmaid's dress from Wallès, 8 rue de Choiseul, is in the Chicago Historical Society (1953.202).

6 The 1894 French edition assumes already established preferences and refrains from including any listings of such services.

7 McCall 1883, p. 2.

8 Ibid., pp. 39–40.

9 Ibid., p. 87.

10 Pingat had turned his business over to Wallès by the time the disastrous tin weighting of silk became an accepted practice. Many twentieth-century Worth and Doucet garments have been ravaged by this chemical treatment, which is a slow killer of silks.

11 It is probable that fabrics associated with the House of Pingat, like the distinctive textiles of Worth, found their way to local dressmakers. A rather severely cut deep plum velvet reception gown, said to have been worn by Mrs. J. B. Lippincott in Oct. 1879, is relieved by a front panel of a stylized Persian-blossom-motif brocade woven in silk and gilt metallic threads in bright, almost garish magenta, hot pink, bright gold, and white (Philadelphia Museum of Art, 50.60.3). In a different colorway, with peacock blue ground and composing part of a later-style promenade ensemble of bodice, skirt, and cape-mantle, the fabric reappears in a garment much less adroitly designed and made (The Brooklyn Museum, 63.212).

12 *The Queen*, Nov. 13, 1880, p. 433.

13 Ibid., Sept. 4, 1880, p. 209.

14 Ibid., July 8, 1882, p. 37; Aug. 18, 1882, p. 173; Sept. 23, 1882, p. 269.

15 Ibid., June 16, 1883, p. 566.

16 Ibid., Aug. 8, 1885, p. 147. The Phoenix Art Museum (1972 c. 531) has a dolman with matching muff dating from the mid-1880s that carries an early gold-stamped label on black moiré.

17 Some clients they are known to have shared are Mrs. Leland Stanford, the Hewitts, Mrs. Augustus Eddy, and Mrs. Henry Adams.

18 No references have yet turned up to theatrical clients.

19 *The Queen*, Aug. 8, 1885, p. 147.

20 Adams Letters, p. 330.

21 Jachimowicz 1978, pp. 47–48.

22 Ross 1963, p. 267.

SELECTED BIBLIOGRAPHY

ADAMS LETTERS [Adams, Mrs. Henry]. *The Letters of Mrs. Henry Adams*. Ed. by Ward Thoron. Boston, 1936.

ADBURGHAM 1961 Adburgham, Alison. *A Punch History of Manners and Modes, 1841–1940*. London, 1961.

ADOLPHUS 1895 Adolphus, F. *Some Memories of Paris*. New York, 1895.

ARNOLD 1985 Arnold, Janet. *Patterns of Fashion: The Art and Construction of Clothes for Men and Women c. 1560–1620*. New York, 1985.

BALSAN 1952 Balsan, Consuelo Vanderbilt. *The Glitter and the Gold*. New York, 1952.

BEERBOHM 1896 Beerbohm, Max. "1880." In *Works of Max Beerbohm*. London, 1896.

BERGER 1982 Berger, Margaret Liebman. *Aline Meyer Liebman, Pioneer Collector and Artist*. Privately printed in U.S., 1982.

BICKNELL 1895 Bicknell, Anna L. *A Life in the Tuileries Under the Second Empire*. New York, 1895.

BLUM 1974 Blum, Stella. *Victorian Fashions and Costumes from Harper's Bazar: 1867–1898*. New York, 1974.

BURNETT 1880 Burnett, Frances Hodgson. *Louisana*. 1880.

CARETTE 1889 Carette, Mme. *My Mistress, the Empress Eugénie; or Life at the Tuileries*. 1889.

CHAPON 1984 Chapon, François. *Mystère et splendeurs de Jacques Doucet: 1853–1929*. Paris, 1984.

DE MARLY 1980a de Marly, Diana. *The History of Haute Couture 1850–1950*. New York, 1980.

DE MARLY 1980b ———. *Worth, Father of Haute Couture*. London, 1980.

DORSEY 1986 Dorsey, Hebe. *The Belle Epoque in the Paris Herald*. London, 1986.

FAWCETT 1881 Fawcett, Edgar. *A Gentleman of Leisure*. Boston, 1881.

GRAMONT 1952 Gramont, Elisabeth de. *La Femme et la robe*. Paris, 1952.

HEGERMANN-LINDENCRONE 1912 Hegermann-Lindencrone, Lillie de. *In the Courts of Memory*. New York, 1912.

HEGERMANN-LINDENCRONE 1914 ———. *The Sunny Side of Diplomatic Life*. New York and London, 1914.

HOLLANDER 1978 Hollander, Anne. *Seeing Through Clothes*. New York, 1978.

HOOPER 1892 Hooper, Lucy. "Worth." *Harper's Bazar*, Jan. 23, 1892.

JACHIMOWICZ 1978 Jachimowicz, Elizabeth. *Eight Chicago Women and Their Fashions 1860–1929*. Chicago Historical Society, Chicago, 1978.

LATOUR 1958 Latour. Anny. *Kings of Fashion. New York, 1958.

LONERGAN 1907 Lonergan, W. F. *Forty Years of Paris*. London, 1907.

LYNES 1981 Lynes, Russell. *More Than Meets the Eye: The History and Collections of the Cooper-Hewitt Museum*. Smithsonian Institution, Washington, D.C., 1981.

McCALL 1883 McCall, James. *French and English Systems of Cutting, Fitting and Basting*. First series. New York, 1883.

MELBA 1925 Melba, Nellie. *Melodies and Memories*. New York, 1925.

MILLAR 1963 Millar, Oliver. *The Tudor, Stuart and Early Georgian Pictures in the Collection of Her Majesty The Queen*. London and Greenwich, Ct., 1963.

NICOLSON 1977 Nicolson, Nigel. *Mary Curzon*. New York, 1977.

OLIPHANT 1878 Oliphant, Mrs. *The Art of Dress*, 1878.

PAGET 1923 Paget, Walburga, Lady. *Embassies of Other Days and Further Recollections*. 3rd ed. London, 1923.

POIRET 1931 Poiret, Paul. *King of Fashion: The Autobiography of Paul Poiret*. Trans. by S. H. Guest. Philadelphia and London, 1931.

RICHARDSON 1971 Richardson, Joanna. *La Vie Parisienne 1852–1870*. New York, 1971.

ROSS 1963 Ross, Ishbel. *Crusades and Crinolines*. New York, 1963.

SALA 1948 Sala, George A. *Paris Herself Again*. Vol. 2. London, 1948.

SHERWOOD 1884a Sherwood, Mrs. John. *Manners and Social Usages*. New York, 1884.

SHERWOOD 1884b Sherwood, Mrs. M. E. W. *The American Code of Manners*. New York, 1884.

SICHEL 1958 Sichel, Pierre. *The Jersey Lily: The Story of the Fabulous Mrs. Langtry*. Englewood Cliffs, N.J., 1958.

STORCH AND MARTIN 1889 Storch, Adrien, and Henri Martin. *Lyon à l'Exposition Universelle de 1889*. Lyon, 1889.

THARP 1965 Tharp, Louise Hall. *Mrs. Jack*. Boston, 1965.

WHARTON 1905 Wharton, Edith. *The House of Mirth*. First published 1905. Ed. cited: New York, 1985.

WHARTON 1920 ———. *The Age of Innocence*. First published 1920. Ed. cited: New York, 1970.

WHITEHURST 1873 Whitehurst, Felix. *Court and Social Life in France under Napoleon III*. London, 1873.

WORTH 1928 Worth, Jean-Philippe. *A Century of Fashion*. Boston, 1928.

PHOTOGRAPH CREDITS